America's First Ladies

❖

BOOKS BY *Diana Dixon Healy*

America's First Ladies   1988
America's Vice-Presidents   1984

America's First Ladies

PRIVATE LIVES OF
THE PRESIDENTIAL WIVES

❖

Diana Dixon Healy

ATHENEUM   *New York*   1988

For my parents

❖

Photographs from the collections of
the Library of Congress, Washington D.C.
Reprinted by permission.

Atheneum
Macmillan Publishing Company
866 Third Avenue, New York, N.Y. 10022
Collier Macmillan Canada, Inc.

Library of Congress-in-Publication Data
Healy, Diana Dixon.
    America's first ladies.
        1. Presidents—United States—Wives—Biography.
I. Title.
E176.2H43 1988   973'.09'92 [B]   88-3365
ISBN 0-689-11873-2

Macmillan books are available at special discounts for bulk purchases
for sales promotions, premiums, fund-raising, or educational use.
For details, contact:

Special Sales Director
Macmillan Publishing Company
866 Third Avenue
New York, N.Y. 10022

10 9 8 7 6 5 4 3 2 1
Printed in the United States of America

Contents

Contents

Contents

vii

Contents

Contents

Preface

❖

A close look at the presidential wives and other women who have served as America's First Ladies over the course of our nation's history provides an interesting perspective on the role of women in our culture as well as their gradually evolving influence on the political scene.

Throughout the first century of our history, a woman's place was firmly in the home, preferably in the kitchen or nursery, and the president's wife was no exception. Families were large and might have been even larger if health care had been better and the infant mortality rate lower. In addition to being breeders, the wives of men prominent in politics were expected to act as hostesses and to be gentle and gracious, in contrast to the coldness so many of their husbands projected to the public.

The early First Ladies lived up to these expectations, though there were a few obvious exceptions; Abigail Adams's personality was too strong and her marriage too much a partnership to allow her to be satisfied with the status quo for women. Sarah Polk, because she had neither children nor any obligation to be a hostess, was able to devote herself to active management of her husband's political career. On the whole, however, most First Ladies in those years limited their White House role to entertaining and decorating, and the style and protocol of each "reign" varied according to the personality and views toward drinking and dancing of the woman in charge.

After the Civil War, constraints on women's activities slowly started to loosen. Early feminists began agitating for change, including the right to vote, greater opportunities for careers and education, and a stronger voice in controlling their own destiny. Although change was wrought at a two-steps-forward, one-step-back pace, the role of women in the White House did expand. First Ladies began to realize the enormous potential in their prominent position and were better prepared intellectually to play an active and positive part in their husbands' administrations.

It seems to come as a surprise to some observers to learn that many First Ladies were influential and competent advisers to their husbands. Indeed, there would probably be a national outcry if a president were publicly to give his wife full credit for anything he had said or done. Yet one may understand why so many First Ladies were able to help their husbands if it were more widely known that the majority of American presidents married above themselves, either socially, financially, or academ-ically. This, perhaps, says something either about the youthful ambitions of these men or their powers of persuasion. It may also indicate the ability of their wives to perceive a bright future for their husbands.

The First Lady has a unique position in Washington; she is unpaid, unelected, and unfettered by rules. She can choose to hide in the executive mansion or to use it as a springboard for a cause. The amorphous nature of the position is what makes it so controversial. If there are no bounds, when is she stepping out of line? If there is no definition of the job, when is she not doing it properly? If her husband is, or appears to be, weak, when is she running the government? First Ladies as different in style as Helen Taft, Edith Wilson, Rosalynn Carter, and Nancy Reagan have all been accused, at one time or another, of wielding excessive power.

And what are we to make of the term "First Lady," which came into popular use during the tenure of Lucy Hayes? Is it necessary for the wife of the president of a democracy to have a title? Would it be disrespectful to just call her "ms" or "missus"? Why don't the spouses of the prime ministers of Canada, England, France, and Australia have titles? Prime spouse? Many First Ladies hated their title; Jacqueline Kennedy thought it made her sound like a "saddle horse." What about the eventual "First Gentleman"; will he stand for it? Without the title, there might be fewer demands for perfection.

The White House experience elicits unpredictable reactions in a First Lady. Many of the early First Ladies found that it was easier just to stay in the private family quarters than to subject themselves to potential criticism.

Some, such as Margaret Taylor and Eliza Johnson, were positive recluses. More recently, Bess Truman, Mamie Eisenhower, and Jacqueline Kennedy tried to maintain a more private, family-oriented posture. Some, Jane Pierce and Mary Lincoln, for example, led a tragic existence in the White House; others, such as Betty Ford, rose above personal problems to become effective spokeswomen for their views and an inspiration for other women. Mrs. Ford's hard-won self-esteem contrasts sharply with that of an earlier First Lady, who titled her autobiography *Adventures of a Nobody*.

Most of the First Ladies have had problems adapting to scrutiny by the public and the media, and tried different ways of dealing with it. Abigail Adams complained that she knew "not how to place so many guards about me, as will be indispensable, to look at every word before I utter it, and to impose a silence upon myself, when I long to talk." Edith Roosevelt expressed the common feeling when she said, "One hates to feel that all one's life is public property." Frances Cleveland had to contend with "keyhole journalism" while on her honeymoon. Helen Taft, who had dearly wanted to be the wife of a president, also felt the discomfort, saying, "The same white light that beats upon a throne sheds its sometimes uncomfortable radiance upon the usually unprepared heads of America's chief executive and his family." Jacqueline Kennedy referred to the omnipresent women reporters as "harpies."

Both Betty Ford and Rosalynn Carter had the experience of being scolded for "sneaking off" for shopping trips in New York without informing the press. Reporters felt they weren't asking too much. As they told Lady

Bird Johnson's press secretary, Liz Carpenter, journalists only ask three things: "Never lie. Tell us you can't tell us, but never lie. Return our phone calls. Don't resent our intrusion. It's our job to know where the First Lady is and what she's doing. We resent being resented."

The press, of course, is just doing what it has to do, which is to tell the public what it wants to know. People care about what the First Family is doing, saying, and wearing. Yet each of these things is subject to misinterpretation or criticism from those who are opposed to the politics of the man in the White House. The more unpopular the president, the more painful it is for his family to read the papers; if he is so popular as to seem untouchable, his wife becomes the lightning rod.

Not only do First Ladies have to contend with the intrusive media, but even in the family quarters there is no real privacy. There is a very large staff up there, and many of them willingly talk about the folks they serve; some have even written books comparing all who have lived in what they come to think of as "their" domain.

Increasingly, our First Lady must live with the possibility that her husband will be assassinated. Lincoln, McKinley, Garfield, and Kennedy were assassinated, and Teddy Roosevelt, Truman, Ford, and Reagan were shot at. Others have died in office, or shortly after leaving it, in what seems to have been a direct result of the rigors of presidential duties.

Despite the problems inherent in being a First Lady, many emerge as dynamic women. Some have been more popular, perhaps even more capable, than their husbands. The changes in the public perception of the presidential wife since the time of Eleanor Roosevelt (and largely because of her) have opened doors as well as added responsibilities for the spouse of the chief executive. It is now expected that the wife of a presidential candidate will campaign with him, and that, once in the White House, she will have a special and worthwhile project. These are usually "soft issues," health or art or gardening projects. They are important matters, but not of interest to every woman. Some have lobbied for legislation to clean up the capital's slums or taken a stand for the rights of women and minorities. Others have tried to stay informed by listening in at cabinet meetings.

Probably no two people would agree on just what the role of a First Lady should be, or who has filled the role most graciously and effectively. The ambiguous quality of the position makes it one of the most unusual challenges a woman can face, both difficult and filled with possibilities. Most of the women who have held the position have put their personal stamp on their husbands' administrations and have in turn been marked by their tenure as First Lady.

Future First Ladies (or Gentlemen) will have to continue to seek that delicate balance between assertiveness and reticence. And changes in the expectations of society will be reflected in the distaff side of the White House in ways that will, one hopes, allow us to more fully appreciate the diversity and capabilities of the women who serve there.

Diana Dixon Healy
Wilton, Connecticut
September 1987

Martha Dandridge Custis Washington 1731–1802

"LADY WASHINGTON"
George Washington Administration 1789–97

❖

With no precedents to either follow or ignore, Martha Washington had the easiest, and perhaps the most challenging, tenure as First Lady. And since there were no guidelines, there was considerable confusion and controversy about exactly how the wife of the first American chief executive should be addressed—"Lady Washington" eventually seemed to stick—how she should dress, and how often and lavishly she should entertain. Having just rid itself of King George III, the new nation was wary of any of the trappings of royalty, but it did not want its conduct to be found vulgar or uncouth to European observers either. Essentially, it was

MARTHA DANDRIDGE CUSTIS WASHINGTON

up to Martha to set the style and tone for the role of the wife of the president. It was not a job she relished, but she had wonderful qualities for it.

Martha Dandridge was born in New Kent County, Virginia, on a plantation in the Tidewater area, the nearest thing the U.S. had to a landed aristocracy. She was the oldest daughter of John and Frances Dandridge. Her education, typical of girls of that time and place, consisted of being "exposed" to books, though not enough to endear them to her or enable her to spell in any standard way. She was much more thoroughly trained in the arts of running a home and dealing with servants; the fine points of knitting, needlework, and sewing; and entertaining the almost constant stream of family and friends who visited.

At seventeen, brown-haired, petite, attractive Martha married Daniel Parke Custis, a wealthy landowner in his thirties. They had four children, two of whom lived. Before their eighth anniversary, Custis died, and Martha was left, at age twenty-five, a wealthy widow. Wealthy young widows were usually not alone for long, and George Washington, a tall, twenty-six-year-old colonel in the Virginia militia, knew a good thing when he saw it. They were married in 1759.

Their prosperous, peaceful life at Mount Vernon, Virginia, was interrupted when George was selected to lead the Continental Army during the Revolutionary War. Martha was supportive of the cause and of her husband. Each winter she joined the general at his headquarters, where she nursed the young wounded soldiers, sewed for them, and tried to raise their morale with her comfortable matronly presence. Tragically, her only son died at the end of the war, and the Washingtons adopted two of his young children and raised them as their own. (Martha's other surviving child with Custis, a daughter, had died as a young girl.)

Back at Mount Vernon after the war, Martha was a constant hostess; so rarely did they dine alone that George was wont to record the occasions in his diary. Some of the guests at his table urged him to head the new government, and finally he assented. This meant taking Martha from her home for another eight years to, as she said, "occupy a place with which many younger and gayer women would be extremely pleased. . . ."

Martha arrived at the nation's temporary capital in New York City a month after George's inauguration. She made the only public statement in her years as First Lady on the way there, when she was so touched by the enthusiasm of the crowds who cheered her as she passed through Philadelphia that she stopped to thank them. The first presidential home, near what is now the Brooklyn Bridge, was where she began what she unaffectionately called the "lost years."

The first presidential reception took place just two days after her arrival. Most of the details of protocol for this event had been decided beforehand—by George, not Martha. The host and hostess wore fine though unostentatious clothes, much to the disappointment of their more glittering guests. The food and drink served was simple fare, and the party came to a somewhat abrupt and early end when Martha announced to the guests that "the General retires at nine o'clock, and I usually precede him. Good night."

This set the pattern for the Washingtons' years as the nation's first couple. Things were formal, somewhat cold, and, as observers admitted later, dull. Martha did what she could to relieve the impression of George's severity and uncommunicativeness (which may have been due, to some extent, to his partial deafness); she smiled at his stories and refused to become involved in political discussions.

Every Tuesday afternoon George hosted a stag party or "levee" wearing full uniform, and Friday evenings Martha received guests—of both sexes—at her "drawing rooms," which George attended as a guest, leaving his sword upstairs. Polite women of the time were expected to return all calls made by those who had visited them, so a great deal of Martha's days were spent dashing about in her carriage returning calling cards. The custom of holding an open house on New Year's Day (one that continued until 1930) started with the first presidential couple.

Democrats like Jefferson considered the Washingtons' receptions too aristocratic, while those more accustomed to European ways thought them too common. Their more elaborate Thursday night dinners for members of Congress were called "an awkward imitation of royalty" by some, while the couple's frank enjoyment of the theater was deemed undignified by others. No wonder the beleaguered First Lady once complained that she felt "more like a state prisoner than anything else; there are certain bounds set for me which I must not depart from—and as I cannot do as I like, I am obstinate and stay at home a great deal."

When the capital was moved to Philadelphia in 1790, things went somewhat better for Martha; their house was larger, and she was near some of their close friends. She even relaxed enough to extend her retirement hour to ten o'clock. During these years, Martha and Abigail Adams, wife of the vice president, formed a long-lasting friendship based on mutual admiration. The First Lady also took an active interest in the marriage plans of James and Dolley Madison.

When the Washingtons turned their duties over to the Adamses and returned to Mount Vernon in 1797, Martha wrote that "the General and I feel like children just released from school or from a hard taskmaster" and she was "cheerful as a cricket." This happiness lasted only two years; when George died, she knew she had "no more trials to pass through."

After George's death, Martha became the completely private person she had always wanted to be; she burned most of his letters to her and moved into a small attic room where she died three years later.

Abigail Smith Adams
1744–1818

"DEAR PARTNER"
John Adams Administration 1797–1801

John and Abigail Adams wanted to be of service to their country, to raise their children to their own high standards, and to manage their property profitably, and so they formed a partnership, one that lasted for fifty-four years. All through those years they talked and wrote to each other constantly (his letters often opened with "Dear Partner") about how well they were meeting their goals, and they were almost always in agreement as to how each of them should function.

They were lucky to have found each other. Young Abigail was tall and slim, with "keen, penetrating" dark eyes, but she seemed a little too bookish and intelligent to many eligible young men; John, however, was impatient with women less intelligent and committed than himself. Abigail, the daughter of Congregationalist Parson and

ABIGAIL SMITH ADAMS

Mrs. William Smith, was tutored at home because of her frail health and learned to love books. From her grandfather Quincy, onetime speaker of the Massachusetts House of Representatives, she learned to love and understand politics. The Smiths would have preferred a respectable clergyman for their daughter, but finally agreed to her marrying the poor young attorney in 1764.

From the very beginning of their marriage, Abigail took part in the struggles of the developing nation. When the couple had been married for just a year, John led a boycott of the Stamp Act, and England closed the law courts in retaliation. This meant that John could not practice law or make a living, but Abigail encouraged him and was adamant, despite the economic hardship it presented, about doing the patriotic rather than the practical thing. John wrote many times of his appreciation of her feelings of duty "such as become the best of women and the best of men."

Unfortunately, he could also be condescending when praising his wife, "whose capacity enabled her to comprehend, and whose pure virtue obliged her to approve the views of her husband." At the time, John's ideas as to what made a good wife were shared by many, including, at times, Abigail herself, who wrote that "however brilliant a woman's talents may be, she ought never to shine at the expense of her husband." Her truer, deeper feelings about a woman's place may have been expressed in other letters urging John to "remember the ladies and be more generous and favorable to them than your ancestors. Do not put such unlimited power into the hands of the husbands." She reminded him that "all men would be tyrants if they could" and warned of a rebellion by the ladies if they had no voice or representation. She very reasonably asked him why he would not "put it out of the power of the vicious and the lawless to use us with cruelty and indignity with impunity. Men of sense in all ages abhor those customs which treat us only as the vassals of your sex."

Throughout the almost ten years that John was away on the country's business, Abigail was managing their farm in Quincy, Massachusetts—hiring tenants, buying land, handling the finances—and raising their four children. So whatever John's expressed opinion of desirable feminine attributes, in the real world his woman had to be independent, resourceful, and diplomatic.

During his long absences, Abigail's letters kept John informed of political maneuverings and public opinion at home and gave advice and encouragement. He once wrote, comparing these letters favorably to the long-winded bombast in the Senate chamber, "Look at Abigail's letters. . . . Why, they were fit to print themselves. . . . There are more good thoughts, fine strokes and mother wit in them than I hear in a whole week."

Abigail was finally able to join John on a government assignment: when he was serving as minister plenipotentiary in France, negotiating treaties with Great Britain, and then as the first American ambassador to Britain (1785–88). Their being together at last made the sacrifices of political life less onerous for both of them, and her tact and charm were assets in the sometimes tense situations that arose between her prickly, cold husband and the often condescending British government.

After their return to the U.S., during John's terms as vice president and then as president (1797–1801), the Adamses were still often apart; Abigail's duties in caring for the farm and family didn't end with her new social obligations in New York, Philadelphia, and, briefly, in the new capital, Washington, D.C. She even missed John's inauguration as president because she was caring for his dying mother.

It is small wonder that, occupied with farm care, worried about family, and often ill herself, Abigail did not relish the additional duties that fall to a president's wife. When she heard that being First Lady was described by one woman as a "splendid misery," Abigail agreed that "she was not far from the truth."

What was much more to her liking was being John's confidante and being able to influence events—a bit too much so according to political opponents. Office-seekers would often address their petitions to her, and she sent articles and letters favorable to her husband's administration to newspapers who then published them. Yet there was always a sort of tug of war waging in Abigail's psyche between what she knew was ladylike (quiet) and what most interested her (politics), so she tried to be quietly political. Her partisanship of the Federalist party, however, was so overt that Pennsylvania Republican Albert Gallatin named her "Mrs. President not of the United States, but of a fraction."

For most of Adams's one term as president, he and Abigail lived in Philadelphia—the nation's new capital was still just a swampy wilderness, "a quagmire after every rain." The mansion in Washington became the official presidential home only after John knew that he had not been reelected. He wanted Abigail to be with him at the end of his term in office, because he knew that she had been an indispensable partner "in all the dangerous consequences we had to hazard." He wrote urging her to join him in Washington for the last three months of his administration, saying that it was "fitting and proper that you and I should retire together." The mansion was damp, cold, and unequipped for daily living, leading to the temporary creation of the nation's most famous laundryroom when Abigail hung her wash to dry in the East Room.

After retiring, the Adamses lived quietly on their farm in Quincy, where Abigail kept busy with family, farming, reading, and writing letters, including a lively correspondence with Thomas Jefferson. She retained her interest in politics until she died in 1818 at the age of seventy-four. Seven years after her death, her son John Quincy, who had been groomed for the position by his parents, became the sixth United States president. Abigail is thus the only woman to have been both the wife and the mother of presidents.

Martha Jefferson Randolph, Jr.
1772–1836

"A DELICATE LIKENESS"
Thomas Jefferson Administration 1801–1809

❖

Thomas Jefferson was already a widower when he became president in 1801, his wife having died in 1782. Martha Skelton had married at seventeen, but was widowed at age nineteen. She married Jefferson when she was twenty-three and died ten years later after giving birth to their sixth child. Only two of these children, Martha (Patsy) and Mary (Molly), lived to adulthood, and each served briefly as their father's hostess.

Patsy was ten years old when her mother died. With her red hair, she was "a delicate likeness of her father," who took her with him when he went to France as minister plenipotentiary. She was enrolled in a convent school, the Abbaye Royale de Panthemont, outside Paris, where she was so happy that, at fifteen, she informed her father that she had decided to become a nun. She and Molly, who had recently joined the family in France, were calmly but quickly withdrawn from the school and returned to their father's fold.

A cousin, Thomas Mann Randolph, Jr., visited Patsy in France, and they were married back home at Monticello, Virginia, when she was seventeen. By the time her father became president, she had borne six children. Both she and Molly, who meanwhile had also married a cousin, John Wayles Eppes, were too busy having and rearing children to spend much time in the executive mansion. However, for seven weeks in the winter of 1802–1803, they did carry out the duties of First Lady. On this occasion, Margaret Bayard Smith, the wife of the publisher of the *National Intelligencer* and an astute social observer, described the sisters:

"Mrs. Eppes is beautiful. Simplicity and timidity personified when in company, but when alone with you of communicative and winning manners. Mrs. Randolph is rather homely . . . but still more interesting than Mrs. E."

The lovely but delicate Molly died in 1804, shortly after giving birth to her third child. The following winter season, Patsy was again in the president's home, and between social duties she managed to produce her eighth child, James Madison Randolph, who was the first child to be born in the executive mansion.

When Jefferson's daughters were not available, Dolley Madison, wife of the then secretary of state, filled in as hostess. Jefferson democratized the executive mansion's approach to entertaining; while the public receptions on July 4 and January 1 remained as permanent fixtures on the mansion's social calendar, he eliminated levees. He ordered the installation of a round dining table to avoid squabbles about seating privileges and also to make the conversation flow more easily. The only rule left standing was "all gentlemen giving precedence to all ladies in passing from one apartment to another." He did not, however, abandon elegance: a French steward and a French chef served fine food and wines.

When Thomas Jefferson completed his term of office, Patsy and her family joined him in retirement at Monticello. She continued to manage her father's household until he died in 1826. Her husband died two years later, and Monticello was so encumbered by debts that the family could not afford to keep it. She spent her remaining years visiting her twelve living children. She died at the home of her oldest son, Thomas Jefferson Randolph, in 1836 at the age of sixty-seven.

Dolley Payne Todd Madison 1768–1849

"LADY PRESIDENTESS"
James Madison Administration 1809–17

❖

Unlike most First Ladies, Dolley Madison remains a familiar figure to Americans, and not just because her name appears on ice-cream products and at least one highway (in Virginia). Present at the formation of the nation, she has become a legend in U.S. history, both as a heroine and a hostess. Schoolchildren are more likely to remember Dolley's actions during the War of 1812 than those of her husband, James Madison. And she defined the role of official hostess, not just for her husband but for the country. Her ability to still charm us over the centuries attests to her special qualities.

Dolley entertained lavishly, and many criticized her for it; one observer referred to the "barbaric grandeur" of

DOLLEY PAYNE TODD MADISON

her parties and receptions. But "Lady Presidentess," as Dolley was known to some of her women friends, almost singlehandedly proved to Europeans that Americans were not all roughnecks and barbarians. And she showed American women that there could be some refinement in what was often a difficult life. Presiding over elegant dinners and receptions, she democratically extended her charm and tact to Federalists and Democrats, men and women, and rich and poor alike. The longevity of her career as a Washington hostess, which lasted beyond the presidential years, also was a factor in her enduring fame.

Dolley Payne was born in Guilford, North Carolina, and raised as a Quaker on a plantation in Scotchtown, Virginia. In 1783, when she was fifteen, her father, John Payne, sold his slaves and moved the family to Philadelphia, then the nation's capital. John did not fare well in the city; his business faltered, and he was disowned by the Quakers for failing to pay his debts. Shortly after, Dolley decided that the time had come to marry the Quaker gentleman who had been patiently wooing her for three years.

She and John Todd were married in 1790, and their son, John, was born two years later. In 1793, yellow fever decimated Philadelphia, and Dolley lost her husband and her infant son, William. She was twenty-five, pretty, and rather gay for a Quaker. Among the "gentlemen [who] would station themselves where they could see her pass" as she went about her errands in the capital was the forty-three-year-old congressman from Virginia, James Madison. Aaron Burr, who had met—and admired—Dolley when he was living in her mother's boardinghouse, introduced them, and First Lady Martha Washington also encouraged James's suit.

The Madisons were married in September 1794. Marriage to a non-Quaker meant that Dolley lost her membership in the Society of Friends. So while the Society lost a member, the capital gained a new hostess. She quickly learned how to entertain and was finally able to indulge her love of fine clothes, though she continued to wear her simple Quaker grays for the morning housework.

When Madison became Jefferson's secretary of state in 1801, the couple moved to the new and still raw capital of Washington, D.C., and lived with the president for their first three months there. Since Jefferson was a widower (as was his vice president, Aaron Burr) and his two daughters were not often in the capital, the wife of the secretary of state became the nation's de facto hostess, both in her own home on F Street and in the presidential mansion. Whenever Jefferson needed a hostess for one of his democratic dos, he would send her a message reading, "Thomas Jefferson begs Mrs. Madison to take care of female friends expected. . . ."

She used wit to blunt the aspersions of such observers as Mrs. Merry, the wife of the British ambassador, who once deplored a dinner at the Madison home as "more like a harvest home supper than the entertainment of a Secretary of State." Mrs. Madison's apparently innocent and unanswerable response was that "the profusion arose from the happy circumstance of the prosperity of our country. I did not hesitate to sacrifice the delicacy of European taste for the less elegant but more liberal fashions of Virginia."

Eight years later, First Lady in her own right, Dolley began her incomparable reign. James was three inches shorter than his handsome wife, weighed less than she did, and was seventeen years older. Washington Irving described her as a "fine, portly, buxom dame who has a smile and a pleasant word for everybody" and him as a "withered little apple-john," but they were just the couple the country needed. He could handle the problems of his office, including the increasing tension with Great Britain, in peace, knowing that Dolley could handle any prickly personality problems and more than made up for his lack of sociability. At dinner parties, it was Dolley who sat at the head of the table, because James didn't want the responsibility of directing the conversation.

At the Madisons' first inaugural ball, Dolley's outfit was described in detail by Margaret Bayard Smith, wife of the *National Intelligencer*'s publisher, Samuel Harrison Smith, for the many women who sought to emulate the First Lady's style, including her use of a small snuff box: "She had on a pale buff-colored velvet, made plain, with a very long train, but not the least trimming, and beautiful pearl necklace, earrings and bracelets. Her head dress was a turban of the same coloured velvet and white satin (from Paris) with two superb plumes, the bird of paradise feathers." Public interest in Dolley's wardrobe continued for the rest of her life, and the feathered turban became her trademark. Yet she was never so bejeweled or glamorous as to arouse envy in other women.

Every Wednesday at the receptions open to everyone, known as "Mrs. Madison's levees" or "squeezes," she had a pleasant word for all even if it meant resorting to a conversational ploy. She would often carry a book around the rooms with her—usually one she had not had time to read—in order "to have something not ungraceful to say, and, if need be, to supply a word of talk." The observant and seemingly omnipresent Mrs. Smith wrote that "Mrs. Madison was a foe to dullness in every form, even when invested with the dignity which high ceremonial could bestow."

On New Year's Day, 1814, the Madisons—she in pink satin trimmed with ermine—gave a lavish reception, and the parties continued, in a determined effort to distract people from the danger of a British invasion, right up to the end of August, when the British advanced through Maryland. As they approached the capital, James rode off to take command of some defending troops, and Dolley was left in charge of the executive mansion, the original draft of the Constitution, the Declaration of Independence, and important cabinet papers. When she was finally forced to flee on August 24, she managed to save the papers and the portrait of George Washington, but the house itself and its furnishings were burned by the British troops, leaving just the outer shell of the mansion.

The Madisons were never again able to live in the presidential mansion but continued to entertain in smaller homes in the city. One of Dolley's more elaborate affairs was given to honor the hero of the War of 1812, General Andrew Jackson, whose life may have been in more danger from the smothering crowds at the reception than during the Battle of New Orleans, the victory of which had won him fame.

After serving eight years in the presidency, the Madisons retired to the family estate in Virginia, Montpelier, where for the next twenty years Dolley was a constantly gracious hostess. The house was seldom without guests, and she never turned away the many people coming to pay their respects to her husband and herself. It was not unusual for dozens of unexpected guests to be given dinner and a place to stay.

When James died in 1836, there was no keeping Dolley down on the plantation; she moved back to the city she loved and her house on Lafayette Square. The Monroe, John Quincy Adams, and Jackson administrations had come and gone, and another bachelor was in the White House. Martin Van Buren did not ask the former First Lady to be his hostess, but she helped him out anyway by playing matchmaker for his son, Abraham, who married a relative of Dolley's, Angelica Singleton, who then served as surrogate First Lady. Later, when the daughter-in-law of the widower Tyler took on the duties of First Lady, Dolley Madison was again on hand to give advice and attention. Sarah Polk assumed a somewhat disinterested role as hostess and would not serve alcohol in the White House, but she was a great friend of the former First Lady across the square, to whom the White House guests would go for stronger drink after leaving the dry company of the Polks.

When Dolley Madison died in the summer of 1849, President Zachary Taylor was the chief mourner among the many officials from all branches of the government. Her legacy as a gracious hostess and her many years of involvement in Washington's social life and with people of all political persuasions have given her a special place in this country's history. When Dolley attended her last presidential reception early in 1849, she was eighty-two years old, still smiling brightly, and still in her satin gown and turban.

Elizabeth Kortright Monroe
1768–1830

"LA BELLE AMÉRICAINE"
James Monroe Administration 1817–25

❖

The eight years of the Monroe administration were known as the Era of Good Feeling, but these feelings did not extend to the distaff side of the presidential household. Elizabeth Monroe was, by most accounts, a lovely woman with dark hair and blue eyes who looked much younger than her years. She also had had ample preparation for her role as the capital's leader of polite society. Yet for all her potential, Elizabeth had a major problem: She had to follow Dolley Madison, and Dolley could not be duplicated.

Elizabeth was born in 1768 in New York City to

ELIZABETH KORTRIGHT MONROE

Hannah and Lawrence Kortright. She met James Monroe when he was serving as Virginia's representative to the Continental Congress in New York. James's political career proceeded to include four terms as governor of Virginia and several years on diplomatic assignments in Europe. The French way of doing things, their clothes and furnishings, became the preferred way for the Monroes, and the French were fond of them, too.

While her husband was serving as the U.S. minister to France, the young Elizabeth endeared herself to the French aristocracy for her part in the rescue of Madame de Lafayette from the guillotine. During the bloodiest days of the French Revolution, Elizabeth courageously went alone in her carriage to visit the imprisoned wife of the man who had meant so much to the American Revolution, and this exhibition of American interest in Madame's fate resulted in her release. As a result, Elizabeth was fondly called "la belle Américaine."

While her husband was serving as Madison's secretary of state, Elizabeth had the opportunity to observe how things were done in Madison's executive mansion, and apparently did not approve of some what she saw. She observed Dolley receiving and returning so many calls that even *her* energy flagged. John Quincy Adams took note of this exhausting practice, saying that Dolley had "subjected herself to this torture which she felt very severely, but from which, having begun the practice, she never found an opportunity of receding." Elizabeth decided not to continue this routine of bucketing about the mud roads of Washington just to leave her card in someone's front hall. This decision earned her great enmity from her contemporaries in the capital, but future First Ladies must have been grateful.

For a long time, the disgruntled women boycotted Elizabeth's "at homes" in retaliation for her curtailed social schedule. One such evening was described by the wife of editor William Seaton: "The drawing room of the President was opened last night to a row of beggarly chairs." And James Fenimore Cooper, with some ingratitude, described an event he had attended as "cold and unimaginative rather than formal" and said that there was "neither any marked exhibition of spirit nor any words of grace."

James Monroe backed his wife on any social changes she wished to make, but the rest of Washington was not so sanguine about what John Quincy Adams called this "senseless war of protocol." And like many others, he put most of the blame on the Monroes' married daughter, Eliza Hay, "an obstinate little firebrand," who had been given much of the responsibility for the social planning in the mansion. It is not clear why Elizabeth gave her daughter so much leeway. It may have been because she herself was in poor health, or perhaps she was unwilling to shoulder all the responsibilities. Or maybe she just wanted to give Eliza a chance to play queen.

Eliza had been raised and educated in Europe and counted as her best friend Hortensia de Beauharnes, a relative of Napoleon and onetime Queen of Holland. Eliza knew that Americans were still considered provincial by European diplomats and may have wanted to make the executive mansion as much like a formal European court as possible, but she was bossy and a stickler for protocol, and many Americans did not appreciate her efforts.

Her unpopularity reached a peak over the affair of her sister's wedding. In 1820, seventeen-year-old Maria Monroe married her cousin Samuel Lawrence Governor, a junior secretary to the president. This was the first wedding of a president's daughter to take place in the executive mansion, and it should have been something grand, but the older sister took charge and decreed that it would be in the "New York style," meaning just family and close friends. Eliza also ruled that since she herself did not call on the wives of diplomats, her sister could not either; diplomats were told to "take no notice of the marriage." This meant that the young newlyweds did not receive gifts from many people from whom they might have been expected.

After a five-day honeymoon, the young couple was allowed to receive guests at a reception in the mansion, and the first of what was to have been a series of balls was given for them at the home of Commodore and Mrs. Stephen Decatur. Unfortunately, Decatur was killed in a duel two days later and all parties were canceled while the capital was in mourning. The Monroe sisters were never close after those sticky social run-ins.

What the Monroe entertainments lacked in warmth and spontaneity was made up for by the richness of the furnishings the couple had purchased for the rebuilt mansion. The presidential residence became known popularly as the White House because, to cover the soot left by the burning in 1814, the building was painted white. Most of the pieces of furniture were imported from

France, and additional expenses were incurred when the seal of Louis XVIII, still imprinted on some of the pieces, had to be removed and replaced with the American eagle. The elegance of all the gilded wood and silk, crystal and bronze, porcelain and satin went on public display on New Year's Day, 1818. It was generally considered very grand and imposing, and a 13½-foot bronze centerpiece is still used on the long table in the White House dining room.

The grandest social event of Monroe's second term was the reception given for the aging hero, the Marquis de Lafayette, on New Year's Day, 1825. Another colorful occasion was a visit by the chiefs of six Indian tribes, all dressed in their rather skimpy native regalia, decorated with beads and brightly painted.

In 1825, aloof, regal Elizabeth Monroe retired with her husband to Oak Hill, their home in Virginia; she died there five years later.

Louisa Johnson Adams
1775–1852

"A BIRD IN A CAGE"
John Quincy Adams Administration 1825–29

❖

A superficial glance at Louisa Adams would reveal a rather sickly unhappy woman, trapped in the White House, with no demonstrable influence on her husband and no set projects of her own. But Louisa happens to have left us an extensive written record of her thoughts, and through them we discover a compassionate concern for the difficult conditions of the women of her time. Louisa realized the futility of seeking independence as a person, even within her own family, but beneath the passive, timid surface there beat the heart of a feminist who admired those strong women who were "what God intended woman to be, before she was cowed by her Master, man."

LOUISA JOHNSON ADAMS

"A Bird in a Cage"

Louisa Johnson, daughter of an American father and an English mother, was born in London, lived in France, and spoke French fluently. She was accomplished on the harp and piano, wrote poetry, and loved to read, especially the classics; she had what she referred to as a "happy but alas visionary education." John Quincy Adams, then minister to the Netherlands, met and became engaged to Louisa on a visit to London. She was slender, blond, pretty, and, most importantly to John Quincy, shorter than he, but their romance was not a grand passion. He gave her a study plan to prepare herself for marriage and told her he would come for her sometime in the next seven years.

They married in 1797 and moved to Berlin, where he was the new American minister to Prussia. During their first thirteen years of marriage, Louisa was pregnant eleven times and bore three children who lived.

In 1801, the couple returned to the States, and John Quincy was elected a U.S. senator from Massachusetts, which meant a gruelling life of commuting between the capital and Boston. Louisa liked Washington but found it difficult to adjust to rigid, puritanical New England, which she admitted was the "land of learning" but not "of wit." Eight years later, Adams was appointed minister to Russia, and he instructed his wife to leave their two oldest sons with family and bring just the baby. When Louisa protested that all preparations had been made "without the slightest consultation," her husband called her concern for the children an "affectation."

St. Petersburg was cold, dark, and uncomfortable; the Adamses lacked the funds to meet their social obligations; and the daughter who was born there soon died.

Louisa was understandably not unhappy to leave this "gaudy loneliness." The exit from Russia proved to be the grand adventure of her life. Thirty years later she wrote of it in a "Narrative of a Journey from Russia to France, 1815." She hoped that the description of her courageous trip would counter "the fancied weakness of feminine imbecility" and demonstrate that things which seemed difficult to women "are by no means so trying as imagination forever depicts them." For Louisa, it remained a memory of a time when she was independent, capable, and alive.

With her six-year-old son Charles, a French maid, and a small Russian military escort, she set out from St. Petersburg to meet John Quincy, who was waiting for them in Paris. Their carriage was fitted with runners to negotiate the icy route, and it was so cold that all their food and wine froze solid. Many times along the way the snow was so deep that local peasants had to be enlisted to dig them out. The party barely made it across the frozen Vistula River in Poland before the ice broke up. When they replaced the runners on the carriage with wheels, they were often delayed by having to repair or replace the wheels that broke on the rough roads. When word reached the group that Napoleon had escaped from Elba and was on the move, the escort unchivalrously deserted Louisa, leaving just a fourteen-year-old boy to guide them through Europe. French troops, often drunk and raucous, mistook the travelers for Russians and threatened them. Once they were nearly dragged out of their carriage and killed, but Louisa had the presence of mind to cry out "Vive Napoleon," and managed to convince the French that she was American.

After several more weeks of arduous travel through Europe, she arrived in Paris. John Quincy had just come from the theater and was somewhat annoyed that she had not arrived on schedule—beyond doubt a difficult man to live with.

For eight years (from 1817 to 1825), John Quincy was Monroe's secretary of state. This position had already become a stepping-stone to the presidency, but it might not have worked that way for Adams without the graciousness of Louisa. Cold, dour John Quincy, left to his own unsocial ways, might have alienated the members of Congress, then responsible for nominating the president. Louisa rose above her own shy nature and entertained often, salon-style in her home. The ball she gave for Andrew Jackson on the tenth anniversary of the Battle of New Orleans was the grandest social event in the election year of 1824. The contest between Adams and Jackson was so close that it had to be decided in Congress. Adams won with some help from Senator Henry Clay, who subsequently was named secretary of state. Charges of corruption persisted throughout the Adams presidency.

From the start, Louisa found the "great unsocial" White House depressing and could not feel at home there. The Monroes had taken much of their furniture with them; what remained was in a somewhat tattered condition. She did what entertaining was necessary, but because of the lingering bitterness of the election John Quincy was a most unpopular president, and the Adamses were often alone together. Both unhappy, they quarreled often, and she complained that their isolation had a "tendency to render us savages."

In an effort to keep busy, she asked friends to send her French books to translate. She wrote poetry and long letters. In one letter to her husband she complained of feeling like "a bird in a cage," brought out only when he needed her to make an appearance. She also objected to "that sense of inferiority which by nature and law" women were made to feel and sardonically told him that it gave as much "satisfaction as the badge of slavery generally." Like many women of the time, she often traveled to spas, less for her health than to escape the demands of her husband.

Through the years, Louisa Adams tried writing her autobiography, titling it according to how she felt about herself at the time, either *Record of a Life* or *Adventures of a Nobody*. In the last years of her life, while John Quincy was serving in Congress, Louisa tried to analyze women's true role by studying the Old Testament, where she found evidence of an intended equality between the sexes. She and women's rights activist Sarah Grimké corresponded frequently on the subject. She also discovered her mother-in-law's letters on women's rights and considered them "treasures." A few years before her death in 1852, Louisa did for a woman slave what she could not do for herself; she bought the woman's title and set her free.

Emily Donelson Donelson 1808–36

"SURROGATE HOSTESS"
Andrew Jackson Administration 1829–37

❖

Rachel Donelson Robards Jackson died a few months before her husband's inauguration in 1829. Many, including Andrew Jackson, attributed her death to a broken heart brought on by attacks on her reputation made during the campaign.

Rachel had moved from Virginia to the Tennessee wilderness when she was twelve and married Lewis Robards at seventeen. Robards had a violently jealous nature, and the couple separated six years later. He told her he was filing for divorce, so she felt free to marry Andrew Jackson in 1791. Two years later, the Jacksons discovered that Robards had not completed the divorce proceedings and was now suing on grounds of adultery. The Jacksons went through another marriage ceremony in 1794, but the gossip and rumors continued, especially among Andrew's political rivals.

The Jacksons had no children of their own but always had a houseful of Rachel's young relatives. In 1809, they adopted Andrew Jackson, Jr., one of twin brothers born to Rachel's fragile sister-in-law. Andrew Donelson, another of Rachel's nephews, was raised in the Jacksons' home, the Hermitage in Nashville, Tennessee. He married his first cousin, Emily Donelson. It was Emily who served as Andrew Jackson's hostess in the White House.

Emily, a slender, titian-haired woman, was just twenty-one when she arrived at the White House. She was the mother of one child and gave birth to three more while there. The president loved having Rachel's young relatives at the mansion and often had parties for them, inviting other children of the capital "for a frolic in the East Room."

The only discord arose when Secretary of War John Eaton married Peggy O'Neal Timberlake, another woman with a tarnished reputation. Andrew, remembering the abuse his own wife had received, defended Peggy, but Washington women, including Emily, refused to call on her. Finally, in frustration, the president sent Emily back to Tennessee. But he missed her and implored her to return—on the condition that "you will do your duty by Mrs. Eaton." The problem was resolved when the president sent Eaton off to serve as governor of Florida. And Emily returned to the White House.

Andrew Jackson built a home, Tulip Grove, for the Donelsons on land adjacent to his estate. In the spring of

1836, while visiting her home, Emily developed rapid tuberculosis and never returned to Washington. She died that December. Sarah Yorke Jackson, the wife of Andrew Jackson, Jr., presided at the White House for the final few months of Jackson's term.

Angelica Singleton Van Buren
1817–78

"QUEENLY SURROGATE"
Martin Van Buren Administration 1837–41

Martin Van Buren's administration began without a woman in the White House. This made many people, including Dolley Madison, uneasy. Americans, and especially Washington society, had come to value, to appreciate, a woman's touch in their executive mansion.

Martin's wife, Hannah, had died in 1819, many years before he became president, and he alone raised their four sons: Abraham, John, Martin, and Smith. From the Senate, he went on to become Andrew Jackson's secretary of state and then vice president, and in 1837, the family of five unmarried Van Burens moved into the White House.

ANGELICA SINGLETON VAN BUREN

This pack of very eligible bachelors was sure of its ability to run a womanless house. They redecorated the mansion with elegance and discouraged the democratic masses from making themselves at home there, as they had in Jackson's time. For their small dinner parties, they brought out the gold spoons and emerald finger bowls and might have managed quite a socially successful administration all by themselves, but ever-popular Dolley Madison thought otherwise.

Angelica Singleton came to the capital to stay with her relative, Senator William Preston, and to visit with her cousin-by-marriage, Dolley. Angelica was a member of a prominent South Carolina family and had attended Madame Greland's school in Philadelphia. Dolley immediately presented her at the White House, where the dark-eyed beauty became a great favorite with the Van Burens, especially Abraham. He was a West Point graduate then serving as his father's private secretary. Abraham and Angelica were married in November 1838.

By New Year's Day, 1839, she was in the receiving line with the president. A reporter from the *Boston Post* described her: "perfectly easy and graceful in her manners, and free and vivacious in her conversation . . . and is said to have borne the fatigue of a three hours' levee with a patience and pleasantry which must be inexhaustible to last one through so severe a trial."

That spring the young couple took a belated honeymoon to Europe, where they were entertained by Queen Victoria in England and King Louis Philippe in France. Angelica seemed to have adopted some of the European ways of entertaining and brought them back to the White House. At levees, she received guests sitting on a dais in a long purple gown and a jeweled headdress sprouting three feathers (always a little longer than other women's).

When Martin Van Buren lost his bid for reelection in 1840, Abraham returned to military service and served in the Mexican War. Angelica dispensed with her queenly manner and returned to her more modest though still elegant nature. They eventually settled in New York City where Angelica died in 1878.

Anna Symmes Harrison 1775–1864

"FRONTIER WOMAN"
William H. Harrison Administration 1841

❖

Anna Harrison was too ill to accompany her husband to his inauguration on March 4, 1841. A few weeks later, as she was packing to go to the capital, she heard that he himself was sick, and before she could set out, she learned that he was dead—exactly one month after taking the oath of office. So we will never know how she would have handled being First Lady.

Anna was the daughter of a New Jersey judge, John Cleves Symmes, and was educated at the Clinton Academy on Long Island and Miss Graham's Boarding School in New York City. When she was nineteen, her father took her from this genteel environment to settle on the

ANNA SYMMES HARRISON

Ohio frontier. She was pretty and petite, with dark hair and dark eyes, and soon attracted young Lieutenant William Henry Harrison. Her father did not approve of his daughter's marrying a soldier because of the hard life she would have in the frontier forts, so the couple eloped in 1795. They had ten children whom Anna educated herself with a little help from traveling tutors.

William served as the congressman from the Northwest Territory and then was appointed governor of the Indiana Territory, a section of the country even farther west. It was a land of unbroken wilderness still subject to Indian attacks. The Harrisons settled on the banks of the Wabash in a settlement called Vincennes, where they built the first brick house, Grouseland, in the region. It was during their time there that William led the army in the successful battle against the Indians at Tippecanoe. He resigned from the army in 1813 and, with his family, settled down to farming in North Bend, Ohio. They added twenty-one rooms onto a log cabin, creating their home, called The Bend, on the Ohio River.

In 1840, the Whigs decided that the hero of Tippecanoe who lived in a "log cabin" was the perfect opponent to run against the dandyish Martin Van Buren. One visitor to the Harrison home described Anna at that time as "one of the handsomest old ladies I ever saw, a perfect beauty, and such a *good* person." She was not sanguine about the prospect of moving to the White House. "I wish," she said, "that my husband's friends had left him where he is, happy and contented in retirement."

She was not able to accompany her husband to the inauguration, so he took a widowed daughter-in-law, four grandchildren, and several other relatives with him to Washington. Within a few weeks, he was stricken with something called "bilious pleurisy" and died. Anna lived for more than twenty years after his death and retained her interest in reading, especially about politics and the history of religion. She was survived by only two children, one of whom was her son John, whose son Benjamin became president in 1889, making Anna the only First Lady to be the grandmother of a president.

Letitia Christian Tyler
1790–1842

"SOUTHERN BELLE"

Julia Gardiner Tyler
1820–89

"ROSE OF LONG ISLAND"
John Tyler Administration 1841–45

John Tyler had two wives during his single term as president. The first, a retiring invalid, he buried in 1842; the second, a lively society woman with regal pretensions, he married in 1844. The women had in common only an unswerving devotion to their husband, and each presented him with seven living children.

LETITIA CHRISTIAN TYLER

JULIA GARDINER TYLER

Letitia Christian was a Southern belle from Virginia, a young woman who believed in all the conventions of the time, acquiesed willingly to the domination of father and then husband, and lived a life of quiet domesticity. After an engagement that lasted nearly five years, she allowed her hand to be kissed by her fiancé, only three weeks before the wedding.

She was happiest when she stood well in the background and appeared only when absolutely necessary during her husband's term as governor of Virginia. One observer wrote of Letitia, "[S]he was perfectly content to be seen only as a part of the existence of her beloved husband; to entertain her neighbors; to sit gently by her child's cradle, reading, knitting or sewing."

Letitia bore nine children, but two died in infancy and her health deteriorated after the loss. In 1838, she suffered a crippling stroke. Still in her forties, she was already "in her declining years and wretched health."

In 1841, John Tyler, who had already made arrangements to spend most of his term as vice president at home, was called to Washington, D.C., to take over the presidency after the sudden death of William Harrison. Letitia felt it was her duty to accompany him to Washington even though she knew she would be unable to function as First Lady. In fact, only once did she leave her room and come downstairs, and that was for the wedding of her daughter Elizabeth in January 1842. Nine months later, Letitia was dead and the capital went into mourning.

If life with Letitia Tyler sounds somewhat stifling to us, perhaps it seemed that way to her widower, too. Certainly his second wife was a complete change for him—and for Washington society. Julia Gardiner was twenty-four when she married the president, who was thirty years older than she. She was also a beauty, known as the "Rose of Long Island." One smitten observer described how her "large gray eyes, raven hair, and the clearest olive complexion, seemed to attract the most eminent men from the time she entered society."

Young Julia had many suitors in her native New York City, and she attracted still more when she and her family toured Europe. While she was traveling, a dry goods company back home paid her the untoward compliment of using her likeness on a handbill in an advertisement for its products.

Her social life became even more exciting when the Gardiner family visited the nation's capital for the winter social season and she had the widowed president flirting with her. Their relationship appeared to take a more serious turn during a cruise on the steamer *Princeton* on February 28, 1844, with a large group of Washingtonians, including the elderly Dolley Madison. As the president chatted with the women guests belowdecks, an experimental cannon exploded during a demonstration on the deck above and killed five men, including the secretary of state, the secretary of the navy, and Julia's father.

Some witnesses swore that John Tyler carried Julia, who had fainted at the news of the accident, down the gangplank. At any rate, it was certain that he wanted very much to console her, and he ordered the funeral for her father and the other victims to be held in the White House. In the wake of the tragedy, the two drew still closer, and, after a brief, secret engagement, they were married at the Church of the Ascension on Fifth Avenue in New York.

Washington society was miffed to miss out on the wedding of the first president to be married in office (a belated reception was held in the Blue Room), but in her eight months as First Lady, Julia more than made up for the loss with a busy schedule of entertaining. Her letters home rang with confidence and a regal attitude: "I have commenced my auspicious reign," she wrote, "and am in quiet possession of the Presidential Mansion." She refused to stand in her reception lines. When guests came, they found her seated on a platform, surrounded by maids of honor, with enough diamonds in her hair to create a crownlike effect.

In a description of one success, she wrote to her family, "Last evening, I had a most brilliant reception. . . . At least fifty members of Congress paid their respects to me and all at one time." She told the folks at home of the compliments "heaped" on her, and then somewhat more modestly conceded, "I suppose I may conclude I looked quite well."

Julia introduced the polka to Washington society and then taught the Marine Band to play "Hail to the Chief" whenever her husband entered the room for official functions. She would have played it herself if she could; there was nothing Tyler did or said with which she found fault. She was so strongly in favor of his annexation of Texas that she wore on a chain around her neck "the immortal gold pen with which the President signed the annexation bill." Until he died, she referred to him as "the President."

When his term ended, the Tylers moved to his Virginia plantation, Sherwood Forest, where she bore their seven children. Julia completely adopted John's Southern sympathies in the increasing tensions between the slave and free states, while alienating her own family in the North.

In 1862, while John was serving in the Confederate Congress in Richmond, Julia had a dream in which he appeared before her with his tie and collar in his hand. Finding this ominous, she rushed to Richmond. He was fine and surprised to see her, but the next morning he did appear just as she had dreamt, then collapsed and died of an apparent heart attack.

By the end of the Civil War, the Tyler estate was in decline and could no longer support Julia and her children. She applied to Congress for and was finally granted (in 1880) a pension of $1,200 a year (increased to $5,000 in 1881), enough for her to live comfortably in Richmond for the rest of her life. It would be almost a hundred years later (1958) before presidential widows received automatic pensions. Julia died in 1889 in the some hotel where John had succumbed and was buried beside him in Richmond. (Letitia had been buried with her parents on the plantation where she was born.)

Sarah Childress Polk
1803–91

"A GREAT DEAL OF SPICE"
James K. Polk Administration 1845–49

Sarah Polk and her husband, James, worked together like a well-oiled machine. He handled the usual male role of running for office and speaking in public, while she set the tone, handled the finances, gave advice in private, fostered the friendships, and, without ceding any of her femininity, prodded him on to higher office. Being childless made it easy for her to travel and read and, finally, to serve as President Polk's official confidential secretary.

The daughter of Captain Joel and Elizabeth Childress, Sarah was raised on a prosperous plantation in Tennessee. She was well educated for a young woman of the time, having attended the Salem Female Academy in North Carolina. Fellow Tennessean Andrew Jackson— "Uncle Andrew" to young Sarah—gave her a taste for

SARAH CHILDRESS POLK

politics and encouraged her romance with James Polk. She urged James to run for the state legislature, and when he won agreed to marry him. The machine was in motion.

A year later, in 1825, James was elected for the first of his fourteen terms in Congress, and his wife was always at his side. Once when she suggested staying in Tennessee to look after their home, he replied, "Why? If it burns down, we can live without it." Without her as his personal assistant and confidante, political life would not have been so smooth for him. He was hardworking but not very personable, while Sarah, in spite of her own industriousness, had many friends and admirers.

Sarah was considered attractive in a dark-eyed Spanish way and dressed in the low-cut gowns fashionable at the time. There were some quiet observers who thought she was the dominant partner in the marriage and showed "a great deal of spice" for a woman, but she contended that everything she did was for the health of her husband. After James's one term as governor of Tennessee (from 1839 to 1841), Sarah felt it would be better for them back in the more exciting atmosphere of Washington, and was gratified when dark horse Polk was elected to the White House in 1844.

As confidential secretary to the president, Sarah resented the time her social life as First Lady demanded. She took little interest in running the White House household or looking after the details of state dinners. She would not return calls and entertained only when necessary. Perhaps her only contribution to the comfort of future White House occupants was to have gaslights installed.

The Polks had strong views on moral conduct, as well as about living within their means. She served no food or drink at the twice-weekly receptions, and she forbade dancing in the mansion, saying, "To dance in these rooms would be undignified, and it would be respectful neither to the house nor to the office." When the Polks walked onto the floor at their inaugural ball, the dancing stopped.

Sarah felt that it would be unladylike to state her own views in public, so she would preface her opinions with the words, "Mr. Polk says. . . ." She was not so gentle with James's detractors, although he didn't seem to be bothered by criticism. Once he ordered an invitation to the White House to be sent to a man Sarah considered unsympathetic to him. She found the invitation before it could be dispatched and burned it. James wrote in his diary that the event amused him.

It was probably fortunate that Sarah had no children and little social life, because James, a loner, had little confidence in members of his staff or cabinet, and he turned more and more to his wife as confidante. And Sarah was always there, believing that her responsibilities were God-given and that the two of them "belonged to the nation." They took the job so seriously that he refused to consider a second term in order to avoid making partisan decisions during the first.

The Mexican War, waged during the Polk administration, had been a huge success for the expansionist plans of the U.S., but it had also been a drain on his stamina. They took only a few days of vacation time in four years and worked such long hours—often staying up late to make up for time spent on social affairs—that Sarah was often ill and James so weak and emaciated that he died within weeks of leaving office.

Sarah survived her husband by forty-two years and spent her time making their Nashville home, Polk Place, a place of pilgrimage. During the Civil War, her political good sense overcame her Southern sympathies, and her home was respected as neutral territory by both North and South.

Margaret Smith Taylor
1788–1852

"POOR WHITE OF THE WILDS"
Zachary Taylor Administration 1849–50

Margaret Taylor did not want her husband to be president and probably prayed harder for his defeat than his opponents did. She felt that his nomination was a "plot to deprive her of his society and shorten his life." It may not have been a plot, but shorten his life it did. The hero of Buena Vista, the decisive battle of the Mexican War, the man who had spent years in the Florida swamps and the Mexican heat, who had served in the frigid fortresses of Wisconsin and Minnesota, could not survive the unhealthy miasma of the nation's capital.

Margaret Smith was born in Maryland to Ann Mackall and Walter Smith. She met young Lieutenant Zachary Taylor in Kentucky where she was visiting her sister, and they were married the following year, 1810. She spent her early married life following Zachary from one primitive, dangerous army post to another. They had five daughters, two of whom died of malaria when young, and one son.

All three daughters married army men, much to the distress of their parents, who knew what a difficult life they would have. The second daughter, Sarah Knox, eloped with West Point graduate Jefferson Davis, who later became the president of the Confederacy, but she died of river fever within three months of the wedding.

In 1848, the Whigs saw the conqueror of Santa Anna in the Mexican War as their ticket to a return to the White House. The new First Lady, then sixty-one years old, unwell, and anxious to settle down with her husband on the Mississippi plantation they had bought for his retirement, considered the move to Washington a punishment. Once in the White House, she spent most of her time in the family quarters upstairs, leaving the entertaining to her daughter Betty Bliss, who was married to Zachary's adjutant.

Washington society resented not having the White House parties to which they felt entitled. The opposition party did not dare attack Taylor, a hero, but took out their frustrations on the invisible mistress of the mansion. She was spoken of as a "poor white of the wilds," too uncouth and uncultured to be seen in polite society. In fact, growing up in a prominent Maryland landowner's family, she had received as much education as most privileged women of the time. Rumors also spread about her proclivity to smoking a corncob pipe in her room; the truth was that tobacco smoke made her "actively ill."

The proof of her gentle, retiring nature might have become known in time, but only fifteen months after coming to the capital, Zachary sickened after sitting for some hours in the sun at the cornerstone-laying ceremonies for the Washington Monument that were held on July 4, 1850. Five days later he was dead. His unhappy widow "lay without uttering a sound, but trembled silently from head to foot as one band after another blared the funeral music."

She lived with her daughter Betty for two more years and died in 1852. Her only memories of her White House years were of the terrible time of her husband's funeral.

Abigail Powers Fillmore
1798–1853

"CREATOR OF THE WHITE HOUSE LIBRARY"
Millard Fillmore Administration 1850–53

❖

Abigail Fillmore knew what was expected of a First Lady; she had become familiar with the capital's customs during the years her husband had served in Congress and his months as vice president. She was a bright, curious, interested woman, and she determined from the beginning of their unexpected propulsion into the White House just how she would conduct herself as the president's wife. Her plans did not include pleasing those Washington natives who felt entitled to a gay social life. Her delicate health, so common in so many women of the day, with the added dimension of an old ankle injury that made standing in reception lines difficult, was excuse enough for her to spend her time more as she pleased.

ABIGAIL POWERS FILLMORE

Abigail was born in Saratoga County, New York, in 1798, the daughter of Baptist minister Lemuel Powers, who died when she was an infant. The family was poor, but with her mother's tutoring and extensive use of her father's library, Abigail had acquired enough education by the time she was sixteen to begin supporting herself by teaching. A few years later, a tall eighteen-year-old named Millard Fillmore entered her classroom wanting to learn. The tall, auburn-haired young teacher taught him, he wooed her, and eight years later they were wed (1826). In an unusual move for brides of that day, Abigail continued to teach for two more years while Millard worked to establish his law practice and rose in the Whig party.

Millard spent several years in Congress while Abigail raised their two children and continued to learn, teaching herself French and music. She still loved reading and enjoyed political and literary discussions with her husband and friends.

When she moved into the White House, Abigail knew that Washington society would have little tolerance for such a bookish, serious hostess, and the excuse of frailty left her peacefully upstairs except for such necessary duties as Tuesday receptions and Friday levees. Much of the job of hostessing was delegated to her eighteen-year-old daughter Abby. However, when an event appealed to Abigail—a Jenny Lind concert or a public banquet honoring Hungarian liberator Kossuth—her health made a marked if temporary improvement, and she broke the unwritten rules against the First Lady's leaving the White House for a public event.

Newly laid water pipes in the capital brought water into the executive mansion for the first time, and Abigail had the first bathtub installed. In the kitchen, she had an iron range put in to replace the open fireplace that had been used for cooking up to then.

Of much more importance was Abigail's installation of a White House library in the upstairs Oval Room. In all the cavernous mansion rooms, the new First Lady had not been able to find so much as a Bible or a dictionary—a deplorable state for Abigail and one that was rectified with a small congressional appropriation enabling her to purchase the works of her favorite authors, including Thackeray and Dickens. Along with her chosen books, she installed her daughter's harp and piano in the Oval Room, making it the most congenial room in the family quarters. There Abigail entertained her close friends with her witty and erudite conversation.

Ignoring the good advice of his wife, Millard signed the Fugitive Slave Act, and it proved to be a political death warrant for the Whigs and for his own chance of reelection. He had agreed to the measure in hopes of preserving the Union by appeasing the South, but the Abolitionist movement was growing, and Northern Whigs began to switch to the new Republican party.

The Fillmores had read much about Europe, and in 1852, they were free to make the trip there. They planned to tour for several months and began to study maps and pack their bags, but first they welcomed the Franklin Pierces to Washington. Abigail gamely took part in all the inaugural ceremonies despite the foul, cold weather and then moved into the Willard Hotel to rest up and recover from a chill. Unfortunately, the chill developed into bronchial pneumonia, and a few weeks later she died in the hotel, within sight of the White House she had been so pleased to leave.

Jane Means Appleton Pierce 1806–63

"SHADOW IN THE WHITE HOUSE"
Franklin Pierce Administration 1853–57

❖

The Pierce tenancy of the White House started under a cloud from which it never fully emerged. When Jane Pierce became First Lady, she was consumptive, worried about her husband's drinking problem, and almost crazed with mourning. Two months before the inauguration, the couple's eleven-year-old son Benjamin was killed before their eyes in a train wreck.

Jane grew up a shy, quiet young woman in a rigidly religious family. She was the daughter of the Reverend Jesse Appleton, a Congregational minister who had been president of Bowdoin College in Maine. When Jane was thirteen the reverend died of tuberculosis, and the

JANE MEANS APPLETON PIERCE

family returned to Amherst, Massachusetts, where she met Franklin Pierce, who was studying law there. The couple did not marry for six years. There seems to have been some family objection to Franklin's interest in politics, which was not considered genteel, and to his drinking with others also interested in politics.

But apparently these differences were sorted out, for Jane and Franklin married in 1834. Franklin, already in Congress, was not yet ready to give up his political dreams, and he was later elected to the Senate. Jane dreaded the little time she did spend in Washington, and constantly badgered her husband to stay at home to practice law in Concord, New Hampshire. Finally, in 1842, Franklin did agree to leave politics and even turned down President Polk's offer of the appointment as attorney general, citing his wife's health as his reason.

During those years, two Pierce sons died, one in infancy and one at the age of four. Jane's health and depression worsened, and she tried even harder to keep her now small family of three together in Concord. But Franklin could not resist the Mexican War; he enlisted and within a year became a general and a war hero. In 1852, as the dark horse candidate of the Northern Democrats, he was elected president. Jane fainted when she heard the news.

A few months later, the three Pierces boarded the train for home at Andover after attending a funeral. The train was running at full speed when the coupling broke and the car in which they were riding plunged down a rocky hill, breaking in two as it fell. Little Benny's forehead was crushed and his face covered in blood when next his mother saw him. She never recovered from the sight.

More than ever now, she resented her husband's ambitions, claiming the boy's death conveniently reduced Franklin's distractions in office. She spent hours in her room writing letters to her dead son and was known as the "shadow in the White House." Her aunt and a friend, Varina Davis, wife of Secretary of War Jefferson Davis, filled in for her as hostess most of the time. When she was able to attend a function, "her woebegone face, with its sunken eyes and skin like yellowed ivory, banished all animation in others."

When Franklin's term in office ended, the Pierces toured Europe for a while. For one winter they tried the Bahamas for Jane's health, but her strongest desire was still to be at home. They returned to Concord where she died in 1863 at the age of fifty-seven.

Harriet Lane
1830–1903

"DEMOCRATIC QUEEN"
James Buchanan Administration 1857–61

After the subdued years of the Taylor, Fillmore, and Pierce administrations, Washingtonians were ready for something—and someone—more lively in the White House. Their wish came true in the fair young form of Harriet Lane. Harriet served as the First Lady for her uncle and legal guardian, the bachelor president James Buchanan. He was sixty-five when he became president. She was only twenty-six when she took over her duties in the executive mansion, but she was so poised, lovely, and gay that she had, among other honors, a song dedicated to her, "Listen to the Mockingbird."

Harriet was the youngest child of Elliot and Jane Lane, both of whom had died by the time Harriet was nine years old. Uncle James, then a senator, was her first choice as guardian. He was not a man known for his

HARRIET LANE

fondness for children, but time would prove her wise in her decision. As a child, "a mischievous romp of a niece" according to James, she was allowed to run free in the Pennsylvania countryside and indulge her tomboyish nature until she and her sister were sent to private school for three years in Charlestown, Virginia. She then attended the Visitation Convent in Georgetown for two years. By the time she was seventeen, Harriet was the hostess of Wheatland, her uncle's home near Lancaster, Pennsylvania, and had already started to master the art of entertaining politicians.

Harriet had thick golden hair and blue eyes, a tall, rounded figure, and was generally thought so attractive that Uncle James ("Nunc" to Harriet) warned her, prior to the first season she spent in the capital, not to succumb to flattery: "Many a clever girl has been spoiled for the useful purposes of life . . . by a winter's gaiety in Washington," he told her. In 1854, James was appointed minister to England and invited his niece to join him in London. She had many suitors abroad and wrote that they were "pleasant, but dreadfully troublesome."

In London, she became a great favorite of Queen Victoria, who bestowed on her formal rank as ambassador's wife. She met Napoleon III and Empress Eugénie when they visited London and was a little "disappointed in the Emperor's appearance. He [was] very short." After dining with the Archbishop of Canterbury, Harriet was loudly cheered by the students as she toured Oxford. Because of all this attention, Nunc once again thought it prudent to warn her, this time advising her "not to display any foreign airs and graces in society at home."

By the time James and Harriet entered the White House in 1857, she was a polished, politically sophisticated, spontaneous hostess, the very model of a "Democratic queen," as she was called. She seated the guests at her dinner parties with a tactful awareness of sectional rivalries and admonished her guests not to discuss politics. She also invited artists to add a touch of culture and arranged to have a greenhouse built onto the executive mansion to provide fresh flowers for the tables.

During what many observers referred to as the "gayest administration," there were at least two White House dinners a week as well as receptions. Women in the capital, happy to have a trend-setter in the mansion again, adopted Harriet's taste for full skirts and low necklines. "Harriet" became a favorite name for baby girls born during her time, and a U.S. steamer was christened the *Harriet Lane*. A young woman less stable or well trained would have been undone by such attentions, but Miss Lane remained natural and unassuming.

Two visits of special interest occurred in 1860. The first Japanese ambassadors ever to visit America arrived. And with their strict sense of protocol, they determined that only Harriet and the cabinet wives were women of sufficiently high rank to be presented to them. The second was the young Prince of Wales, later Edward VII, who was a more relaxed guest. Because the president did not approve of dances in the White House, Harriet invited her younger friends to join her on a cruise, in the ship named for her, up the Potomac to Mount Vernon. Dancing was acceptable on the *Harriet Lane*.

The Buchanan administration was plagued by the apparently insoluble problems between North and

South, and James was grateful for Harriet's tact and political astuteness; she became his "confidante in all matters political and personal." Harriet will be remembered by many as a cheerful, diplomatic young White House hostess during the difficult times just before the Civil War. By the time she and James left Washington in 1861, seven states had seceded and both of them seemed relieved to leave the cares of the violent years for someone else to handle.

The pair lived quietly at Wheatland, Harriet taking seriously Nunc's injunction not to rush "precipitately into matrimonial connexions." Then in 1866, she married Henry E. Johnston of Baltimore, Maryland, and bore him two sons. When her uncle died three years later, Harriet inherited Wheatland, and she and her husband made it their country home. In 1881, their older son died at age fourteen; the younger son died the following year. Two years later, Harriet was a widow with no known living relatives.

She spent the rest of her life living in Washington, where she had known such happy times, and traveling in Europe. She also began collecting art, including such favorites as Sir Joshua Reynolds, George Romney, and Sir Thomas Lawrence. When she died in 1903, Harriet left her collection to the Smithsonian Institution, and it became the basis of the National Collection of Fine Art.

This woman who had been orphaned herself, then lost her only two children when they were youngsters, left the bulk of her estate as an endowment for the Harriet Lane Outpatient Clinic, a home for invalid children that is still in service today as part of the Johns Hopkins Hospital in Baltimore.

Mary Todd Lincoln
1818–82

"A TRAGIC FIGURE"
Abraham Lincoln Administration 1861–65

"He is to be President of the United States some day; if I had not thought so I never would have married him, for you can see he is not pretty. But look at him. Doesn't he look as if he would make a magnificent President?" Thus several years before the fact, Mary Lincoln, who had always considered herself somewhat of a psychic, predicted the future of her husband. For the country, it was fortuitous; for Mary, it was a disaster.

Her life was one of tragedy almost from the day of her husband's election to the presidency, but there were few sympathetic voices raised on her behalf. As newspaperwoman Laura Redden wrote, "It would have been quite impossible, under any circumstances, for her to have satisfied the opposing factions of the day."

MARY TODD LINCOLN

"A Tragic Figure"

Mary Todd came from a wealthy, genteel family in Lexington, Kentucky. Her father, Robert Todd, spoiled his seven children; he gave all of them the best education money could buy and an early exposure to the political world, which included his friend Senator Henry Clay of Kentucky. When Mary was six, her mother, Eliza, died in childbirth, and life was never the same. A new stepmother added eight more children to the family, and in the competition for attention, Mary's swiftly shifting moods became more apparent.

A cousin once described Mary's appearance at about the time she was twenty-one, when she first met Abraham Lincoln, then a struggling country lawyer. She wrote of Mary's blue eyes, dark hair, and bright expression, adding, "Her form was fine, and no old master ever modeled a more perfect arm and hand." Mary was then living with her married sister in Springfield, Illinois. Gay, flirtatious, and sometimes sharply sarcastic, she was able to see the potential in the gawky, moody Abe. He was attracted by her "wit and fascinated with her quick sagacity, her will, her nature and culture." Two years later, in 1842, they were married in spite of her family's objections to his humble background.

In their first eleven years of marriage, four sons were born, one of whom died at four. Over the years the Lincolns developed ways of dealing with each other's moods. She tried to improve his clothes and manners, and he learned that it was sometimes best to take the children and leave the house until one of her temper tantrums had run its course. He took the outbursts with great patience, explaining, "It does her lots of good and it doesn't hurt me a bit."

Abraham served a term in the U.S. Congress from 1847 to 1849. He ran for the Senate in 1858 against Stephen Douglas, the incumbent. Lincoln lost, but became so well-known through his debates with Douglas during that campaign that he became the Republican party nominee for president in 1860. This time he won.

Mary could not have become First Lady under worse circumstances. She was, in the eyes of the society women of the capital—and for many other East Coast sophisticates—a rube from the barely civilized state of Illinois. No matter how she dressed or decorated the White House or entertained, she would not be good enough for the capital's hard-core critics. If she did entertain, they said she shouldn't in wartime; if she didn't, she wasn't doing her duty. If she wore elegant, expensive clothes she was called a spendthrift, anything more plain was subject to ridicule. Not only was she a plump, dowdy little Springfield housewife, but she was married to a man numerous critics referred to as a baboon, a man who admitted to having split logs and to having had little formal education. To make matters worse, during the war, the White House occupants were subject to intense scrutiny.

Unfortunately, Mary was her own worst enemy. Impulsive, imprudent, jealous, emotionally immature, and probably suffering some menopausal problems, Mary was also subject to severe migraine headaches that became more disabling as she grew older. Her hysterics, obsessions, and violent mood swings were recognized by those closest to her as symptoms of mental illness. On hearing of one incident, Abe had to admit, "The caprices of Mrs. Lincoln, I am satisfied, are the result of partial insanity."

One of Mary's first acts in Washington was to hire a mulatto woman, Mrs. Elizabeth Keckley, as her dressmaker. Mrs. Keckley gave the troubled First Lady much sympathetic support. Mary had warned her from the first that "I cannot afford to be extravagant," but she became one of the most prodigious spenders ever to be First Lady. Shopping became an obsession that continued no matter what else was happening. She explained to Mrs. Keckley that she "must dress in costly materials" because of the "critical curiosity" of the people, and her shopping sprees continued all through the war.

Mary's spending went beyond her personal items. The $20,000 Congress allocated for redoing the White House was not nearly enough, so there were huge bills owed to merchants. She had bought two sets of Haviland china—one for the White House, one for herself—a seven-hundred-piece set of Bohemian cut glass, specially made carpets, curtains, and wallpapers for the many rooms of the executive mansion. Her husband was shocked when he discovered how much had been spent for "flub dubs for this_____old house, when soldiers cannot have blankets."

Mary's position in the Civil War was doubly difficult because she was from a Southern slave state (even though it remained in the Union), and most of her family was either fighting for or supporting the Confederacy. Northerners accused her of at least sympathizing with the South and possibly of committing such outright treasonous acts as sending messages through the lines to the Confederate Army. When she failed to secure passes for her Southern relatives or their goods to pass through military lines, they called her a traitor.

The truth is Mary was more of an abolitionist at heart than her husband. As a young girl, she had seen slaves being sold and had heard of the conditions they suffered. Her relationship with the slaves in her family's home was one of mutual affection, and she was always popular with blacks she knew.

On days when the First Lady didn't read about her shopping sprees or treasonous activities, she might see a newspaper story about how unfair it was that her oldest son was not yet in the army. Robert Lincoln and his father both felt that he should be in the service, but concern for Mary's mental health had increased after her favorite son, Willy, had died of typhoid fever in the White House in 1862. Mary was so overcome with grief she could not attend his funeral and would never again go into the room where he had died, nor the Green Room where he had been embalmed. She worried her sister by insisting that the "visitations" she had with Willy at night, following his death, were of some comfort to her. She could not bear the thought that Robert might die in battle, but she allowed him to be assigned a minor staff position in General Grant's army headquarters, where he was unlikely to be exposed to Confederate bullets.

When she had recovered enough from Willy's death to leave her seclusion in the White House, Mary began to visit the wounded soldiers in local hospitals, bringing them fresh fruit and words of hope. Such deeds seldom received attention in print. Mary's young secretary, William Stoddard, with a positively modern grasp on the art of public relations, suggested that it "would sweeten the contents of many journals and of the secretaries' waste-baskets" if she were to take reporters with her to listen to everything she said in the hospitals and then invite them back for cake and coffee.

By the end of 1864, the North was so close to victory that Lincoln was easily reelected, and Mary celebrated by buying a $2,000 gown for the inaugural ball. However, both she and Abe were showing signs of strain and weariness. Always a jealous woman—despite the fact that Abe was devoted to her—that spring Mary, for the first time, lost control in public. While visiting the front, she became incensed at the sight of General Edward Ord's lovely wife riding beside Lincoln during a review of the troops. When Mrs. Ord rode over to say hello to the First Lady, Mary drove the poor woman to tears by greeting her with abusive language and name calling.

General Grant's wife, Julia, who had witnessed this and other scenes, declined an invitation to accompany the Lincolns to see *Our American Cousin* at Ford's Theatre on April 14. That night, sitting in their theater box, her hand resting in her husband's, Mary saw her husband shot and mortally wounded. He died the next morning, and Mary was never again completely rational.

The Widow Lincoln was hounded by the press and by creditors. Among other things, she was accused of taking White House property when she left the capital, and later ridiculed when she tried to sell her White House gowns in New York to raise money. In 1868, her old friend Elizabeth Keckley published a book that described, in embarrassing detail, life with the Lincolns.

That year Mary and her youngest son, Tad, left for Europe where they wandered from city to city for four years.

When Tad died of pleurisy at eighteen, Mary's grip on reality slipped completely. She carried on conversations with imaginary people and spent thousands of dollars on jewelry and other little luxuries that she never used. Finally, to protect her from herself, her son Robert had her declared insane and committed to the Bellevue sanitarium in Batavia, Illinois, in 1875. With the support of her sister and friends, she was released after just four months. She wandered quietly around Europe for a few years, then returned to her sister's house in Springfield, where she died in 1882.

Eliza McCardle Johnson
1810–76

"TUTOR TO A PRESIDENT"
Andrew Johnson Administration 1865–69

❖

Eliza Johnson's sojourn in the White House was, for her, both unexpected and unwelcome. She was too weakened by tuberculosis to take an active role as First Lady, and she feared that her unpopular husband would also be assassinated. It would have been difficult for anyone to follow Abe Lincoln as president; it was almost impossible for Andrew Johnson. He was considered a drunkard by many who had seen his stumbling performance when he was sworn in as vice president, and some even suspected him as a fellow conspirator in Lincoln's assassination.

The Johnsons are rare in the annals of first families in that they both came from great poverty and were

ELIZA McCARDLE JOHNSON

married while still in their teens. Eliza's father, John McCardle, was a shoemaker in Greeneville, Tennessee, who died when she was young. Her mother, Sarah, in spite of limited means, saw to it that her daughter had a basic education. In the Tennessee hills at that time, a knowledge of the basics was sufficient to allow Eliza to become a teacher. After their marriage in 1827, the barely literate Andrew was Eliza's only student; she tutored him while he practiced his trade as a tailor.

Finally, Andrew took everything he had learned from his wife, and leaving her behind with their five children and the financial worries, made his way up the political ladder from the state to the national legislature, from the governorship to the vice presidency. While he was serving as the military governor during the Civil War, the secessionist sympathizers in the state seized "traitor Johnson's" home, forcing Eliza and her children out. It took them months of wandering and hardship before they could reach Andrew in Nashville, and Eliza never regained her health.

As First Lady, Eliza settled in on the second floor of the White House with her reading and needlework, surrounded by her family of two sons; a widowed daughter; the oldest daughter, Martha Johnson Patterson, wife of a senator; and five grandchildren. Eliza may have come downstairs for two or three functions, but left the rest of the duties to Martha, who was well liked for her simplicity and honesty. As she explained her position on entertaining, "We are plain people from the mountains of Tennessee, brought here through a national calamity. We trust too much will not be expected of us." Congress did not allot much money for fixing up the presidential mansion, but Martha freshened the look by covering the worn furniture and rugs with white linen and filling the rooms with flowers.

The Johnson family's calm optimism and simple lifestyle continued right through the impeachment proceedings against Andrew. The charges against him were brought by Republican radicals who were unhappy with his lenient policies for reconstruction in the South. Eliza may have seemed to be invisible in the capital, but she received daily reports on how the trial was going. When Andrew was acquitted by only one vote, the First Lady received the news gratefully, exclaiming, "I knew he'd be acquitted; I knew it."

Six years after they left the White House, Eliza rejoiced in Andrew's complete vindication and reelection to the Senate. Unfortunately, he died the same year, 1875, and she died a year later.

Julia Dent Grant
1826–1902

"A GARDEN SPOT OF ORCHIDS"
Ulysses S. Grant Administration 1869–77

❖

There have been First Ladies who just tolerated being in the White House and others for whom it was a torment. For Julia Grant, life in the presidential mansion was "a feast of cleverness and wit" and seemed to her "a garden spot of orchids." The eight years she spent there were, by her own admission, the happiest in her life and would have been extended to twelve or more if she could have arranged it.

Julia Dent grew up in an atmosphere of privilege and plenty at White Haven, the family's large estate near St. Louis, Missouri. The Dents were slave owners, and her father, "Colonel" Frederick Dent, continued to defend the Confederacy all through the war and even after, in the years he spent living with the Grants in the White House. Young Julia was a tomboy and physically strong

JULIA DENT GRANT

with a will to match. When she met her brother's handsome West Point roommate, Ulysses Grant, she set her heart on marrying him despite her family's opposition to a man who seemed to have few prospects. In August 1848, after a four-year engagement, during which he went off to fight in the Mexican War, they were married.

Life was not easy for the Grants; he seemed to be unable to succeed at anything that was nonmilitary—farming or working in his father's leather goods shop—and the family was often nearly destitute. Through all the hard times, though, the bonds of affection between Ulysses and Julia and between them and their four children remained strong. Then the Civil War broke out, and Ulysses returned to the army. Though a disaster for the rest of the nation, it brought an end to the Grants' financial difficulties and led them to the White House.

Throughout the war, the Grants were never very far apart. Julia followed her husband and often took the children to live with him at his headquarters. This was not just for the sake of family togetherness, she also had a stabilizing effect on him and kept him from his periodic binges with alcohol. There was no love lost, however, between Julia Grant and Mary Lincoln, who visited the headquarters with the president toward the end of the war. Jealous of most women, the First Lady once snapped at the general's wife, "I suppose you think you'll get to the White House yourself, don't you." When Julia claimed satisfaction with her present situation, Mary shot back, "Oh, you had better take it if you can get it. 'Tis very nice."

After leading the North to victory, Grant was so popular that he was almost guaranteed the presidential election, and in 1868 he did win it, telling his wife, "And now, my dear, I hope you're satisfied." She was very satisfied.

The new First Lady was not an attractive woman. She had a dumpy figure and strabismus in her right eye (it was crossed and wandered up and down involuntarily); when she suggested having an operation to correct her eye's placement, Ulysses vetoed the plan, insisting that that was the way he fell in love with her and that's the way he wanted her to stay.

Julia endeared herself to the other Washington women by inviting the wives of senators and cabinet members to stand with her in reception lines. This was not entirely a selfless act on her part; with her poor vision, she needed their help in identifying the guests passing through the line.

The Grant family brought a warmth and informality to the White House. The two older boys were away at college, but young Nellie and Jesse livened up the mansion, and stories of the two cantankerous grandfathers, one an unregenerate Confederate, the other a confirmed Yankee, sniping at each other, amused Washington society.

One observer wrote that there had never been "so little formality or so much genuine sociability in the day-receptions at the White House." Ben Poore, a social commentator of the time, described one of Julia Grant's unpretentious afternoon open houses this way: "There were ladies from Paris in elegant attire and ladies from the interior in calico; ladies whose cheeks were tinted with rouge, and others whose faces were weather-bronzed by outdoor work . . . chambermaids elbowed countesses, and all enjoyed themselves."

First Lady Grant also did well with the more formal state dinners. Her first move toward success was to replace the army quartermaster her husband had installed in the kitchen with an Italian steward who added the touch of elegant food preparation the White House needed. Their weekly state dinners usually consisted of some twenty-five courses and lasted a good two hours. Afterward, there was fifteen minutes of talk in the Blue or Red room before the Grants said good night and went to bed. There was no entertainment, but after spending so much time at the dinner table, most guests were probably anxious either to go to bed themselves or to go for a long walk.

For their second inaugural party, Julia had a special structure erected in Judiciary Square. It was lined with white muslin and known as the "Muslin Palace," but it was so cold that night and so little heat was provided that women had to dance in their wraps, and one poor woman with a bronchial infection collapsed and died on the dance floor. Cages with hundreds of canaries had been hung in the cavernous room, but the birds were too cold to sing.

In 1873, the First Lady made some permanent structural changes in the White House, remodeling it with Grecian columns; she also added plush furnishings, enormous chandeliers, gilded wallpapers, and other gaudy excesses of the Victorian era. Despite increasing attention paid to the first family by the press, there was little criticism of Julia's spending; in the Gilded Age, everyone was doing it.

By May 1874, the refurnished East Room was ready for what was probably the most elaborate production of the Grant years, the wedding ceremony of young Nellie to the Englishman Algernon Sartoris. Expensive wedding gifts covered several tables in the room where they had been put for viewing, while in the East Room the air was thick with the scent of flowers. A wedding bell of roses and baby's breath hung over the couple taking their vows. Unfortunately, the marriage was not happy and ended in divorce seventeen years later.

The eight years of the Grant administration were filled with scandal involving the corrupt appointees of the too-trusting president. It was also the time of stock exchange failures and the Custer massacre, but none of these facts seemed to diminish the popularity of the Grants. Julia had hoped that Ulysses would be nominated for a third term, then resigned herself to leaving the White House so as not to deter "others from enjoying the same privilege." To help her recover from the loss, the Grants took a two-year tour of much of the world—Europe, Egypt, India, China, and Japan—where they were treated like royalty.

Once back in this country and living in New York, Ulysses' inability to make a success of civilian life was again apparent. He borrowed heavily to invest in a brokerage firm that failed, and within three years he lost everything. By then he was dying of cancer of the throat, and he once more looked to the military life to save the family from financial disaster. He spent his last years racing to complete his memoirs of the war years. They were well written and sold well, leaving his widow financially secure.

When Ulysses died in 1885, Julia moved back to Washington, where she was joined by her divorced daughter and three grandchildren. The former First Lady decided to try her own hand at memoirs, but she lacked her husband's lucid style, and the book found no publisher in her lifetime. But in 1975 the book was published, and in it she voiced her strong opinions about those men who had taken advantage of her politically naive but honest husband.

Julia died in 1902 and was laid beside her husband in Grant's Tomb, the monument dedicated to him in 1827 in New York City. This fact might be worth remembering when next responding to the shopworn riddle, "Who is buried in Grant's tomb?"

Lucy Ware Webb Hayes
1831–89

"MOTHER LUCY"
Rutherford B. Hayes Administration 1877–81

❖

The period following the Civil War became known as the "New Woman Era." Opportunities for women were slowly opening up in education and politics. Two movements—women's suffrage and temperance—also afforded females a chance to take a stand, and even to take to the streets. Lucy Hayes in many ways exemplified this "new woman": she was our first college-educated First Lady; she advocated temperance; and she was enthusiastic about politics. However, the early sympathies she expressed for women's rights were tempered by a realization that the country was not ready to give women the vote.

LUCY WARE WEBB HAYES

Born in Chillicothe, Ohio, Lucy Ware Webb was two years old when her father, Dr. James Webb, died of cholera during a trip to arrange passage to Liberia, Africa, for his freed slaves. Her mother moved the family to Delaware, Ohio, so that Lucy's two older brothers could attend Ohio Wesleyan where Lucy was also trained. At sixteen, she began her college education at the Wesleyan Female College in Cincinnati, and by the time she was graduated two years later, her courtship by local attorney and family friend, Rutherford Hayes, was in full swing. They were married in 1852. Over the next twenty years, their union produced eight children, three of whom died as infants.

During the Civil War, Rutherford led the 23rd Ohio Regiment. When he was wounded in 1862, Lucy went to Maryland to nurse him, then stayed on to care for the enlisted men, who called her "Mother Lucy." One of their favorite stories was of the time a raw young recruit needed to have his shirt mended. The more hardened soldiers, knowing that Lucy was in the camp, sent him to see the "seamstress" in Colonel Hayes's tent. They hung about outside waiting for a laugh, but were surprised when the newcomer returned. He ruined their joke when he told them that a woman in the colonel's tent—Lucy herself, though she had not bothered to identify herself—had willingly fixed his shirt.

Even before the war was over, Rutherford was elected to Congress, then to three terms as the governor of Ohio. As the governor's wife, Lucy worked for the establishment of a home for orphans of the state's veterans and visited prisons and asylums with her husband.

In 1876, Lucy became First Lady, a title that was just beginning to be widely used in print by reporter Mary Clemmer Ames in her "Woman's Letter from Washington" column to describe the president's wife. Rutherford had been elected president in one of the country's most controversial elections. His opponent, Samuel Tilden, had won more popular votes, but Hayes won in the electoral college. When even some of the electorial votes were questioned, it took a congressional commission to settle it in Hayes's favor. Because the election was so close and hotly contested, the inaugural ceremonies were simple—a torchlight parade instead of a ball and procession.

Coming after the luxurious but corrupt Grant years, it seemed a refreshing change to many to have a teetotaling, hymn-singing family in the White House; to the more sophisticated, they were four dull years. Lucy was a great favorite of the press; one journalist gushed that she was the "most idolized woman in America." They admired her strong features, large eyes, and Mona Lisa–like expression. She wore her dark hair pulled back in a simple style without the extra "rats" used by other women, and she eschewed the more grotesque bustles and the deep décolletage of the time.

Shortly after the Hayes family moved into the White House, there was a state dinner for Russian Grand Dukes Alexis and Constantin. Everything had already been arranged and the presidential couple was told that it would be necessary to serve wine for diplomatic reasons. Some gossips claimed that there was a drunken incident that evening, but whatever the reason, no more wine flowed in the state dining room after that. Rutherford had taken the pledge as a young man and felt that temperance suited the dignity of the executive mansion (especially since he had seen "noble minds rendered unfit to be trusted in public office because of drink").

It was Lucy, however, who took the brunt of the abuse for running a dry household in a town that probably appreciated a drink at the end of a long day more than most. She didn't proselytize or object to the use of liquor for medicinal purposes; she just did not serve it to her guests. She was ridiculed in newspapers and editorial cartoons as "Lemonade Lucy" who ran a "cold-water regimen." One wag pointed out that "water flows like wine in the White House." There was even a rumor that she was too parsimonious to spend money for wine. However, the Women's Christian Temperance Union, which was formed in 1874 and was to become a strong national influence, supported Lucy to the point of veneration; it arranged to have her portrait by Daniel Huntington presented to the White House.

There were some guests who whispered it about that White House caterers sympathetic to the wets would sneak in a course of "a punch or sherbet into which as much rum was crowded as it could contain without being altogether liquid." Rutherford later explained that this was just a flavoring, but whoever was right, it seemed to make those longing for alcohol feel better.

Lucy Hayes found living in the White House a joy. She once exclaimed to friends as she guided them through the mansion, "No matter what they build, they'll never build any rooms like these." She replaced the billiards room with a second conservatory so that she would always have enough flowers to send to friends, hospitals, orphanages, and kind reporters. More practically, running water came to town and was extended to the White House bathrooms, and an early telephone was installed. To add to the White House china collection, Lucy ordered a dinner service painted with American flora and fauna.

When members of Congress became tired of crunching over broken eggshells, they closed the Capitol grounds to the annual Easter egg roll. Lucy invited the children to use the White House lawn for the event, and a now familiar tradition was born.

She was also sympathetic to the poor in the capital who wrote asking her assistance, and hundreds of dollars' worth of food and other supplies went from the mansion to those in need. She endeared herself to the White House clerical staff by inviting them with their families to Thanksgiving dinner.

For years, evening receptions at the White House had been open to anyone who wanted to attend, including those whose primary interest had been to acquire a souvenir, such as a crystal pendant from a chandelier or a piece of lace cut from the curtains. Lucy tried to prevent this by having the receptions by invitation only. The brilliance of one of her receptions was described by one reporter as being "never excelled in any *fete* given by any administration." And this, obviously, was not whiskey talking.

One of the happiest memories for the Hayeses of their years in the White House was the celebration of their silver wedding anniversary in December 1877. Lucy wore her original bridal gown, with the seams let out to accommodate her 5-foot-4½-inch, 161-pound frame, and they renewed their vows before the minister who had married them twenty-five years earlier.

After four years in the White House, the Hayeses retired to their home, Spiegel Grove, in Freemont, Ohio, where Lucy continued her interest in child welfare. She died in 1889.

Lucretia Rudolph Garfield
1832–1918

"WHITE HOUSE SCHOLAR"
James A. Garfield Administration 1881

❖

Lucretia Garfield was in the White House too briefly to become well known to the public. There is some doubt how much of her personality she would have revealed in any case. Her Victorian-style marriage of twenty-three years had pretty much squashed her own early objections to "submission" and silence.

An intelligent person, she received a good education at the Western Reserve Eclectic Institute in Hiram, Ohio, a school founded with the assistance of her father, Zebulon Rudolph, by the religious group Disciples of Christ. Here she attracted the attention of fellow student James Garfield. Lucretia was an attractive, slender woman with

LUCRETIA RUDOLPH GARFIELD

dark eyes and finely chiseled features, but James seemed more interested in her intellectual gifts. After finishing school, Lucretia took up teaching. She and James had an on-and-off relationship for eight years, during which he continued to woo other women. He wrote to "Crete," expressing concern about her "notions concerning the relation between the sexes," and she tried to reconcile giving up her independence as a teacher for a marriage based on duty. They were finally married in 1858.

Things did not go smoothly for the newlyweds. They were more often apart than together as he attended the state legislature, served in the Union Army (1861–63), and then went to the capital as a congressman. During this time, he also apparently had an affair with another woman. Lucretia described James's dalliance as "lawless passion," but she forgave him for it anyway. The Garfields might have continued with their separate lives if the deaths of two children had not brought them closer together. James became more willing to settle into his role as a family man, and they bought a home in Washington, D.C., where they lived with their five surviving children for the almost twenty years he served in Congress. Lucretia continued with her intellectual and literary interests and had obviously learned to be a good politician's wife. James once paid her the compliment of saying that she was "so prudent that I have never been diverted from my work for one minute to take up any mistakes of hers."

When Lucretia learned that her husband was the dark horse presidential candidate of the Republican party in 1880, she worried that it was "a terrible responsibility to come to him and to me." As First Lady, Lucretia showed more interest in researching the history of the White House in order to authentically restore it than she did in entertaining there. She gave the necessary dinners and held twice-weekly receptions but spent most of her time at the Library of Congress reading over documents pertaining to the old mansion. There was little time for either activity, however; two months after the inauguration, she was stricken with malaria and moved to the New Jersey seaside to escape the unhealthy air in Washington.

On July 2, 1881, while she was still convalescing in New Jersey, James was shot twice by crazed assassin Charles Guiteau at the Washington train depot. He managed to cling to life for almost three months with Lucretia—"frail, fatigued, desperate, but firm"—by his side. When he died in September, she returned to Ohio where she spent the next thirty-six years supervising the preservation of the records of her husband's career. She died in 1918 while wintering in South Pasadena, California.

Mary Arthur McElroy

"NOT QUITE THE FIRST LADY"
Chester A. Arthur Administration 1881–85

❖

Chester Arthur's wife, Ellen, died in January 1880, the year Arthur was elected vice president. When he succeeded to the presidency a year later, he was still mourning her death and would not allow anyone else to take a position of social precedence in the White House.

Arthur's younger sister, Mary Arthur McElroy, accompanied him to the capital to care for his nine-year-old daughter, Nellie—along with her own two daughters— and she assumed some social duties. However, it was Chester himself who set the tone for the White House entertaining. Dinners were formal and lavish; bouquets of roses were presented to the women, boutonnieres to the men. Mary stood in receiving lines with her brother, but often had as many as forty other women accompanying her, diluting her status.

Arthur was a fastidious man of elegant tastes who refused to move into the White House, which he described as "a badly kept barracks," until it had been redecorated to his standards. He hired Louis Comfort Tiffany of stained glass fame as his decorator. By New Year's Day, 1882, the mansion was painted and furnished to Chester's satisfaction and opened to the public. That spring, the citizens of Washington were invited to a once-in-a-lifetime auction at which twenty-four wagon loads of old furniture and "junk" were put up for sale. Among the items sold were Nellie Grant's globe from her school days, children's high chairs from the time of Lucy Hayes, and Abe Lincoln's trousers and silk hat.

Arthur's administration was the only one not to have had even a temporary surrogate First Lady. He was a fine and generous host, knew how to furnish a home in luxurious style, and paid particular attention to his wardrobe (he once ordered twenty-five pairs of trousers at one time). However, the average citizen apparently did not think these interests suitable for a president—at least not one without an official hostess—and he was not reelected.

Frances Folsom Cleveland
1864–1947

"WHITE HOUSE BRIDE"
Grover Cleveland Administration
1885–89, 1893–97

❖

On June 2, 1886, twenty-one-year-old Frances Folsom married President Grover Cleveland in the Blue Room of the White House. It was the first—and, so far, remains the only—wedding of an American president to take place in the executive mansion. The marriage of the lovely, dark-haired, statuesque, recent college graduate to a man twenty-seven years older and almost two hundred pounds heavier was fascinating stuff to the American public and, especially, the press. The wedding ceremony began with the "Wedding March," played by the Marine Band and led by John Philip Sousa, and ended with a twenty-one-gun salute and the ringing of all the city's church bells.

FRANCES FOLSOM CLEVELAND

Grover Cleveland was a gruff man, more comfortable in the company of male political types than in elegant drawing rooms. His private life was not without its shadows; he almost lost the election in 1884 when it was revealed that he had an illegitimate son by one Widow Halprin. However, the dubious financial dealings of the Republican candidate James Blaine seemed more scandalous to the electorate, and the bachelor won.

Grover's younger unmarried sister, Rose, agreed to act as his hostess, though she was accustomed to more intellectual activities. She was a teacher and the author of a study of George Eliot, which had strong feminist ideas. She once remarked that her method of dealing with tedious reception lines at the White House was to conjugate Greek verbs in her head.

As is usually the case with a bachelor, there was much speculation and guessing about the president's marital plans, but when questioned about them, Grover just compounded the mystery by replying, "I'm waiting for my wife to grow up." In fact, the future First Lady was growing up in Buffalo, New York. She was the daughter of Grover's former law partner, Oscar Folsom, who had died when Frances was eleven years old. Though not legally her guardian, Grover, as administrator of her father's estate, took an active role in Frances's upbringing and education.

When "Frank" (as he called her) was at Wells College, "Uncle Cleve" (as she called him) began writing and sending flowers to her. Mrs. Folsom acted as chaperone when they were together, and it was the mother, not the young daughter, who was perceived as the president's romantic interest. Grover capped the training of his future wife by arranging for her to tour Europe after graduation. He must have been satisfied with the way she had turned out, for he wrote to Rose that "I have set my heart upon making Frank a sensible domestic American wife and would be pleased *not* to hear her spoken of as 'The First Lady of the Land' or 'The Mistress of the White House.' . . . I should feel very much afflicted if she gets many notions in her head. But I think she is pretty level-headed."

Frances Cleveland had to be very level-headed indeed to be able to handle the spotlight that was directed at her. After the wedding, what was then referred to as "Paul Pry" journalism began for the Clevelands. Reporters, avidly curious about the young bride, followed the newlyweds to their honeymoon spot in Maryland's Blue Ridge Mountains and set themselves up with their binoculars and cameras in a pavilion a few hundred yards from the newlyweds' cottage. The papers carried detailed descriptions of their every meal, the mail they received, what they wore, and where they walked. The more respectable newspapers deplored this "keyhole journalism."

Grover complained to a friend that he could see the "animals" sitting and waiting "for some movement to be made which will furnish an incident." After the honeymoon, reporters continued to follow the First Lady on her trips to New York City and Buffalo, so upsetting the president that he spoke out against "those ghouls of the press" at a Harvard graduation dinner.

When political opponents began spreading rumors that Frances was abused by her husband and unhappy in her marriage, the First Lady publicly responded that she wished "the women in our Country no greater blessing than that their home and lives may be as happy, and their husbands may be as kind, attentive, considerate and affectionate as mine." To escape the pressures of being in the White House, the Clevelands spent as much time as they could at Oak View, their country home near Georgetown.

Frances turned out to be a great asset to her husband. She was an attractive, unaffected, and charming hostess who enjoyed her social responsibilities even when, after shaking thousands of hands, she had to have her aching arms massaged. She held two receptions a week, scheduling one on Saturday so that the women who worked in the Washington offices could attend. She did not drink herself, but did not force her views on guests and always offered wine at White House dinners.

When Grover was defeated for reelection in 1888, Frances—with amazing confidence—told the saddened White House staff, "Take good care of the house, for we are coming back just four years from today."

When they did return after a four-year hiatus, it was a first in election history, and when Frances gave birth in 1893 to their second daughter, Esther, in the White House, it was another first for this First Lady. The public was so distracted by the newborn baby in Washington that they were unaware for several years that, at about the same time, Grover had submitted to an operation for cancer of the mouth. Doctors performed the operation, removing part of his jaw and palate, in great secrecy aboard a yacht on the East River in New York, then explained the padding around the fake jawbone as an offshoot of routine dental work.

Another daughter was born in the White House before the Clevelands retired to Princeton, New Jersey, where two sons were born. Grover died in 1908, and five years later, Frances became the first First Lady to remarry when she wed Princeton archaeology professor Thomas Preston, Jr. She was involved with the University Women's Club, and during World War I headed the National Security League's Speakers' Bureau and the Needlework Guild of America. When she died in 1947, she was still regarded as a role model for women in the White House.

Caroline Scott Harrison
1832–92

**"BEST HOUSEKEEPER THE WHITE
HOUSE HAD EVER KNOWN"**
Benjamin Harrison Administration 1889–93

Caroline Harrison was publicly praised as the "best
housekeeper the White House has ever known." At the
turn of the century, this was no doubt intended as a great
compliment. However, Caroline was interested in more
than making her home tidy and comfortable. She was
well read, artistic, musically talented, and, as she revealed with her plans for expanding the White House,
well ahead of her time.

Caroline was born in 1832 to Mary Neal and Dr. John
W. Scott, a Presbyterian minister and founder of the
Oxford Female Institute in Oxford, Ohio. She was a
vivacious teenager who was more interested in dancing
than domestic activities. She enrolled at Farmers' College, a preparatory school in Cincinnati where her father

CAROLINE SCOTT HARRISON

was teaching, and met Benjamin Harrison there. Ben saw her as "charming and loveable, petite and a little plump, with soft brown eyes and a wealth of beautiful brown hair."

They were married in 1853, while Benjamin was studying law, and for a time they lived with his grandmother, Anna Symmes Harrison, widow of the former president, William Harrison. During the Civil War, Benjamin enlisted on the side of the North and rose in the ranks. His success at the Battle of Peach Tree Creek, just outside Atlanta, earned him the rank of brigadier general, and he came home to Indianapolis a hero. Meanwhile, Caroline had been raising their two children, Russell and Mary (Mamie), on her own, teaching Sunday school, and giving classes in china painting and needlework.

Well liked for her enthusiasm and warmth, she was a considerable contrast in personality to her husband. This stiff, reserved man, who hated small talk and rode roughshod over his subordinates, would bleed ice water if pricked, it was said, and was "as glacial as a Siberian stripped of his furs."

For all that, he won election to the U.S. Senate. After serving one term, Benjamin won the presidency in 1889, and the Harrisons moved into the White House. Shortly after the election, Caroline expressed her feelings about the new life-syle: "If there is one thing above another I detest and have detested all my days it is being made a circus of, and that is what has come to me in my old age, as it were. I've been a show, the whole family's been a show since Mr. Harrison was elected. All last fall I sat in my sewing room and watched the procession of feet pass across the parlor floor wearing their path into the nap, and disappear like the trail of a caravan into the general's room beyond. Day by day, I watched the path grow wider and deeper, and at last the caravan spread out and engulfed us all. But I don't propose to be made a circus of forever! If there's any privacy to be found in the White House, I propose to find it and preserve it."

Caroline and Benjamin brought their whole "extended family" to the White House: her father, their son and daughter with their spouses, and three grandchildren. Grandson Benjamin Harrison (or "Baby") McKee was one of the most photographed children ever in the White House at a time when photography was just becoming a popular pastime. Various other relatives were also there in different stages of permanent residence, and all these people had to be accommodated in five bedrooms with one bathroom. It is not surprising that Caroline wanted the office moved out of the upstairs quarters so that the family could have more space and some privacy.

To this end, she worked with architect Fred D. Owen on a plan that would extend the White House with wings on either side, the east for office space, the west as the "historic art wing." An enormous conservatory would stretch across, connecting these wings, creating a courtyard in the center. Caroline had hoped to have this project completed by October 1892, the centennial of the White House. Another plan would have an entirely new residence built for the president's family, leaving the White House to the tourists, presidential staff, and favor-seekers. To none of these plans would Congress agree, and it was not until 1902 that the much needed enlargement was made on a modified scale.

With the $35,000 she was appropriated, Caroline tackled the very basic changes that had to be made. First there was the problem of rats. Rats had pretty much been having their own way throughout the cavernous White House basement for some time, even coming up into the dining room if that seemed to be the most likely place for a snack. Caroline fought back by bringing in trained dogs and ferrets, which tracked down and killed hundreds of the brazen rodents.

When she went to inspect the cellar, she found conditions ideal for the rodent family but far too dirty and unsanitary for her own. In the kitchen, several layers of old rotten flooring were ripped up and replaced with concrete and tile, and the tile was extended up to replace the greasy walls. Modern new equipment was then installed.

Her most important utilitarian project was probably the installation of electricity throughout the mansion, even though the Harrisons were too worried about getting a shock to use the light switches themselves. Young Ike Hoover supervised the electrical installation and was still at the White House as chief usher forty-two years later. If he or another member of the staff was not at hand to turn off the lights, they burned all night.

While flinging herself into these major housekeeping projects, Caroline found something much closer to her heart with which to become involved. While installing a new china closet, she discovered the china purchased by First Ladies of many past administrations, from the Monroes to the Clevelands, identified it, and began the extensive china collection that exists today. Artistic herself, she enjoyed painting on china like many women of the time and even taught a course on it while First Lady. She designed a pattern of flowers and cornstalks for use in her own time in the White House.

Caroline filled the conservatories with her favorite flowers, orchids, and initiated the custom of putting up a White House Christmas tree, which was decorated by family and staff, in the upstairs Oval Room.

In 1890, when the Sons of the Revolution refused to admit women even if they could prove there were Revolutionary heroes in their ancestry, the Daughters of the Revolution (DAR) was formed, and Caroline was named its first president general. After she died, the DAR commissioned a posthumous portrait of her by Daniel Huntington and presented it to the White House in 1894.

As First Lady, Caroline remained active in charity work and agreed to help raise funds for the Johns Hopkins Medical School in Baltimore, Maryland, on the condition that it admit women.

During the last year of the Harrison administration, Caroline was often too ill to take part in social activities, and on October 25, 1892, she died in the White House of what was probably tuberculosis. Services were held in the East Room, and the Harrison family sadly went through the motions for the last months of Benjamin's term. He had lost all desire to run again. He retired to Indianapolis where, three years later, he married his wife's widowed niece.

Ida Saxton McKinley
1847–1907

"WHITE HOUSE INVALID"
William McKinley Administration 1897–1901

❖

Ida McKinley became an invalid long before she entered the White House, but she was determined to participate in the ceremonial duties of a First Lady despite her afflictions. Her major health problem, then called a "nervous disorder" or "fainting spells," is now known to have been epilepsy, but at the turn of the century, epilepsy was considered a taboo subject and was never mentioned by the McKinleys or their guests.

Ida was born in Canton, Ohio, the daughter of a prominent local banker, James Saxton. She was lively and outgoing as a young girl and given a finishing-school education followed by a grand tour of Europe. On her return, she studied banking with her father and went to work as a cashier in his bank, an unusual decision for a well-to-do young woman of the time. She met William

IDA SAXTON MCKINLEY

McKinley when he moved to Canton to start his law practice. He thought she was "the most beautiful girl you ever saw" with her blue eyes and auburn hair. They were married in 1871.

Married life was idyllic at first, as the McKinleys settled into the house given to them by the Saxtons, and Ida bore two daughters. The birth of her second child, however, left her permanently weakened. Then, within a few years of each other, her mother and her two young daughters died. From that time, the once vivacious woman was an invalid, subject to periodic epileptic attacks.

William remained devoted to his wife. Some observers felt he was a martyr or a saint because of his constant attention to her demands. He may have had problems at home, but his political career did not suffer for them. He served for fourteen years in Congress and was then elected governor of Ohio. The McKinleys lived in a hotel room across from the capitol in Columbus. Twice a day, William would wave to Ida from the governor's office then watch for her answer—the waving of a white lace handkerchief.

When William was elected president in 1897, his wife presciently exclaimed, "Oh, Major, they will kill you. . . ." Ida may have had forebodings about going to the White House, but she was determined not to let her precarious health keep her in the background—it is said that she spent $10,000 on her wardrobe as First Lady.

Adjustments in protocol and customs were necessary to accommodate the First Lady's health. When Ida fainted at the inaugural ball, William quietly took her from the room until she could recover. Whenever she accompanied him to a function in the capital, special arrangements had to be made to ensure that she could be removed in case of an emergency. The usual seating at state dinners was changed so that Ida could sit next to William. If she had an attack at the table, he would drape his handkerchief over her face and continue his conversation with the guests until the attack passed. At formal receptions, Ida received guests seated in her blue velvet chair and held a bouquet so she would not have to shake hands. Her relatives and the wives of cabinet members assisted her in her duties.

Frail and desiccated-looking, Ida was said to be petulant and demanding. Unlike other First Ladies who had been sickly, she did not choose to remain upstairs in the family quarters and was known to call her husband out of meetings to discuss something trivial. A congressman's wife who had visited the White House provided this description of her: "She sat propped with pillows in a high armchair with her back to the light. Her color was ghastly, and it was wicked to have dressed her in bright blue velvet with a front of hard white satin spangled with gold. Her poor relaxed hands, holding some pitiful knitting, rested on her lap as if too weak to lift their weight of diamond rings, and her pretty gray hair is cut short as if she had had typhoid fever. She shook hands with us lightly, but didn't speak."

William had some difficult decisions to make during his administration; he was being pressured to declare war on Spain in Cuba but tried to avoid it. Even while wrestling with these problems, he took the time to read to his wife and spent as much time with her as possible.

When he went to the Buffalo Exposition in 1901 in upstate New York, Ida insisted on going with him. She was resting in the home of the exposition's president when the news came that her husband had been shot and mortally wounded by a Polish anarchist. His dying words had been: "My wife—be careful . . . how you tell her—oh, be careful."

Ida returned to Canton, where she lived with her younger sister for six years. When she died, she was entombed with her husband in the McKinley Memorial Mausoleum in Canton.

Edith Kermit Carow Roosevelt
1861–1948

"SEVEN YEARS . . . WITHOUT MAKING
A MISTAKE"
Theodore Roosevelt Administration 1901–1909

❖

In the eyes of her adoring husband, Edith Roosevelt
was "the ideal lady and mistress of the White House."
The dreary sickroom atmosphere of the McKinley administration had ended abruptly with McKinley's assassination in 1901, and the energetic young Roosevelt
family swept into the executive mansion and into the
hearts of the American people. Edith was a reserved,
dignified woman, an aristocrat by breeding and upbringing who knew innately how things should be done and
how to make guests feel at home.

EDITH KERMIT CAROW ROOSEVELT

The daughter of Charles and Gertrude Tyler Carow, Edith had many illustrious ancestors, including the early Puritan Jonathan Edwards. She had known Theodore Roosevelt all her life; her family lived next door to his grandfather on Union Square in New York, and "Edie" and Theodore ("Thee") were often together during their summer stays at Oyster Bay on Long Island. The tall, long-faced young woman had patrician good looks but was more interested in books than in whether her dark hair had again escaped its pins and was flying about her face.

To many of their friends, Edith and Teddy had seemed to be near an engagement, but during his junior year at Harvard, Theodore fell in love with Alice Lee. They married and lived happily in New York, socializing in a circle of friends that included Edith. Two years later, Alice died in childbirth. In another room in the house on the same day, Teddy's mother also died.

Three years later, in 1886, Teddy and Edith were married in London, and he never mentioned his first wife to anyone again. (Edith once remarked that Alice would have bored Teddy to death eventually anyway.) Edith was determined to be a good mother to little Alice, who felt closer to her stepmother than she did to her father. Four sons—Theodore, Kermit, Archie, and Quentin— and another daughter—Ethel—came along, and even as First Lady, Edith hoped to add another child to the family.

Teddy spent many years in public service, including time as the police commissioner in New York City and as governor of New York State, before becoming William McKinley's vice president in 1900. Edith was game for anything new Teddy wanted to do, and he valued her judgment of people. In fact, their daughter once claimed, they "all knew that the person who had the long head in politics was Mother."

Edith would probably have asserted that she was first and foremost a wife and mother, and she was. The exuberant and energetic Teddy sometimes needed her strong hand to curb his excesses. Historian Henry James was witness to the effect a gentle look or quiet word from her had on the president and claimed, with his cynical hyperbole, that Teddy stood "in such abject terror of Edith."

Edith preferred to run the White House with her own high standards rather than depend on a professional housekeeper. This meant she took responsibility for maintaining about thirty rooms and planning all receptions and public functions. Under her direction were two cooks, a kitchen maid, two butlers, a pantry man, a steward, her own two maids, a governess and children's nurse, cleaning men for each floor, several men whose only job was to polish floors, ushers, a fireman for making fires in all the fireplaces, and all the other workers in the stables, garden, and laundry.

The job sounds onerous, but Edith loved her years in the White House and claimed that she was one of the few happy First Ladies. One reason for her happiness may have been that the presidential salary was now $50,000, and that, with other recent appropriations, made it possible for her to entertain as she pleased. Her entertainment was divided into three groups: the smart set, the politicians, and the true friends.

A look at a few weeks of the White House calendar would demonstrate just what a busy hostess Edith was. December 18, 1902, was the night for the first annual cabinet dinner; on January 1, 1903, there was a New Year's reception; and weekly after that came the Diplomatic Reception, the Diplomatic Corps dinner, the Judicial Reception, the Supreme Court Dinner, the Congressional Reception, and the Army and Navy Reception. During that time there were also balls, musicales, suppers, and one of the biggest affairs in the mansion, the coming-out party of Alice Roosevelt. At these large receptions, with sometimes thousands of people passing through the receiving line, Edith found that she could avoid having her hand crushed by constant shaking if she held a bouquet in both hands and just smiled as the guests passed by.

During the season in the capital, Edith hosted musicales on Tuesdays and Fridays. On these occasions, following dinner for twenty at eight o'clock, hundreds of guests would arrive for performances by such artists as pianist Ignace Jan Paderewski, the Vienna Male Voice Choir, the Philadelphia Orchestra, and cellist Pablo Casals who, sixty years later, would play the White House again for the Kennedys.

There were garden parties with bands playing and marquees filled with food, and state banquets featuring orchids and champagne. At one memorable lunch in 1905, the guests included historian Henry Adams, stained-glass artist John La Farge, sculptor Augustus Saint-Gaudens, and novelist Henry James.

In spite of the fullness of her social calendar, Edith's

personality did not change; she retained what Teddy's valet called the "kind of distinction you see in few people but which you recognize the moment you see it." She refused to spend large amounts of money on clothes and felt complimented when Mrs. Stuyvesant Fish of New York's high society said, "The wife of the President, it is said, dresses on $300 a year, and she looks it." Edith also retained her high standards of moral behavior in a city not known for its principled conduct; she once went out to lunch rather than stay and meet the well-known womanizer, Russian Grand Duke Boris.

Along with six Roosevelt children, the White House was home to a collection of pets that included the usual dogs and cats, a kangaroo rat that Archie carried in his pocket, and a calico pony named Algonquin. Quentin once smuggled Algonquin up the White House elevator to Archie's sickroom figuring that the sight of the pony would have a curative effect on his brother.

With so many children, animals, and guests on the premises, there was a crying need for more room. Congress appropriated more than $500,000 for improvements and expansion. Construction of the east and west wings, joined to the main house by colonnades, as Jefferson had originally planned it, was the major project. Plumbing and lighting were also modernized. Superfluous architectural additions, along with much of the Victorian fustiness that had been added over the years, were removed.

With the executive offices located in the new wings, there was a separation of living and working quarters, and Edith was finally able to protect the privacy of her family. To keep reporters from hounding the place, she supplied them with current photographs of herself and the children at regular intervals. She gave them access to White House affairs from time to time, but essentially shielded the children from excessive attention.

On February 17, 1906, Alice Roosevelt was married to Congressman Nicholas Longworth of Ohio in the East Room of the White House in an elegant ceremony. There was a reception for almost seven hundred people, at which Alice, always the individualist, showed guests that it was faster—and more fun—to cut a wedding cake with a military sword than with a cake knife. Almost two years later, shortly before the Roosevelts left Washington, Ethel's debut was held in the presidential mansion. She was a little young, only seventeen, but her mother could not pass up such a setting for her daughter's coming of age.

For the newly expanded White House dining room, Edith had had to buy a new set of china. In doing so, she became interested in the collected pieces from previous administrations, which Caroline Harrison had carefully preserved, and Edith arranged to put them on permanent display. She also felt that the old custom of selling or giving away broken or chipped china pieces was undignified and ordered them destroyed instead. She then had a complete inventory made of all White House objects, so that they would no longer be disposed of at the whim of the mansion's current resident, as had happened so often in the past. And in one ground-floor corridor she created a portrait gallery of First Ladies.

When the Roosevelts left Washington in 1909, Teddy's aide, Archie Butt, fondly claimed that Edith had spent "seven years in the White House without making a mistake." Many Americans were as sorry to see this lively family leave as the family was to go; being in the White House had been a high point that would never be equaled, and Edith was certain that "no family ever enjoyed the White House more than we."

The Roosevelts returned to Sagamore Hill, their home at Oyster Bay on Long Island, where they continued to receive guests and lead busy lives. Four years later, Teddy, disillusioned with his friend Taft in the White House, ran against him for president as head of the Bull Moose party, but the Democrats defeated both of them. Edith lost her youngest son, Quentin, in World War I, and Teddy died in 1919 of a coronary embolism.

Edith spent her years as a widow traveling around the world on what she called her "Odyssey of a Grandmother," and she wrote a book about the Carow family, *American Backlogs*. She gave generously to charities, Teddy's Rough Riders, churches, and others in need. She died in 1948 at the age of eighty-seven.

Helen Herron Taft
1861–1943

"PRESIDENT-MAKER"
William H. Taft Administration 1909–13

Helen Taft was a president-maker. At the end of the nineteenth century, it was difficult for women to achieve positions of power, and no one even dreamed it might be possible for a woman to enter the White House as anything other than the wife of a president. Yet the White House was where Helen wanted to be. She was a determined, ambitious, and intelligent woman who, because she could not be a political leader herself, became her husband's mentor and spur.

Helen, or "Nellie," one of eleven children of prominent Cincinnati Republican John Williamson and Harriet Collins Herron was petite with dark hair and a stubborn mouth who looked attractive in her fine clothes. She was not much interested in a social life; one family member described her as being "not a girl of many

HELEN HERRON TAFT

friends nor one who makes them easily." She was, however, an avid reader of history and an outstanding student. When not doing the domestic tasks required of her, she read Thomas Carlyle, a Scottish essayist and historian, and, later, organized a salon for the discussion of literature, music, history, and philosophy. At Miami University of Ohio, she studied German and chemistry. One of her ambitions was to write a book on one of the many subjects that interested her, something which would sell well so that she would not be dependent on anyone for support. To further this dream of independence, she took a job teaching at a private school in a nearby town.

Nellie's other ambition was formed when she was seventeen years old and went with her family to visit the Rutherford B. Hayes family, then in the White House. After that one visit, she was so impressed by the mansion's powerful aura that she swore she would only marry a man "destined to be president of the United States." And these were the words of a woman who did not treat many subjects lightly, especially her own future.

She must have been a young woman of rare perception, because she saw in a plump, easygoing young Cincinnati attorney, recently graduated from Yale, the potential to make it to the presidency. William Howard Taft was not without ambition himself; he wanted to become a judge and, one day perhaps, sit on the Supreme Court. But he was a malleable person, always seeking approval from friends and, especially, from his demanding parents. His mother had feminist leanings, so William learned early in life what it was like to live with a strong woman. In 1886, after a two-year courtship, during which he knew that Nellie deemed his strongest words of praise to be for her "intellectual superiority," they were married. Her own frustrated ambitions were then put on the hefty shoulders of her husband.

When William was only twenty-nine he was appointed a judge of Cincinnati's superior court. He was quite content with this, but when he was offered the position of United States solicitor general, Nellie was relieved that he could leave the "awful groove" of the judiciary and enter politics. Against his will, he accepted the post, and they moved to Washington. Then, as Nellie confessed, William had "an opportunity for exactly the kind of work I wished him to do."

While in the capital, Theodore Roosevelt became William's beloved friend and idol. The Tafts also met other politicians, and Nellie delighted in cultivating allies in high places. After only two years in Washington, they returned to Ohio, where William served as circuit judge for eight years. Nellie must have begun to despair; she had wanted him to have "a diverse experience which would give him an all round professional development"; William, on the other hand, "did not share this feeling in any way." During this time in Ohio, she threw herself into local cultural affairs and was instrumental in establishing the Cincinnati Symphony Orchestra.

When William was asked to head the commission to govern the Philippines, recently relinquished to U.S. control by Spain, Nellie was overjoyed. In spite of the potential dangers to the family, she knew that she "didn't want to miss a big and novel experience." She was not about to let him refuse the offer, and he soon became the first American civil governor.

When Teddy Roosevelt became president, he offered William the position of his dreams: appointment to the Supreme Court. But Nellie and the Filipinos, who liked him, convinced Taft there was still work to be done, and he stayed on. She was much happier with the offer of the post of secretary of war, writing that this was "the kind of career I wanted for him and expected him to have." He accepted and the Tafts moved back to Washington. Again, William was offered the highest court, and again Helen fought it and won. She even went to Roosevelt to explain her views, including her hope that William would be the president's heir-apparent in 1908. Roosevelt agreed to support Taft's candidacy.

Poor Taft. He hated campaigning ("Politics when I am in it makes me sick"), was a dull and ponderous speaker, and dreaded the thought of being president ("Any party which would nominate me would make a great mistake"). Putting him in the White House was the accomplishment of a very strong-minded woman.

On inauguration day, Nellie felt "a little secret elation in thinking that [she] was doing something which no woman had ever done before." She insisted that she ride beside her husband in the carriage down Pennsylvania Avenue to the White House after the swearing in. Exiting President Roosevelt, who would normally have accompanied Taft, had already left town. She took her duties as the president's wife very seriously, and claimed that she was even beginning to neglect politics, explaining, "Perhaps with my husband safely elected, I

considered all important affairs satisfactorily settled. . . ."

Many visitors to the White House felt that Nellie had
not withdrawn enough, and noted how she would
manage to insert herself into her husband's important
conversations and meetings. William was also influenced
when his wife had something to say about political
appointments, as when she insisted that he fire Henry
White, the ambassador to France, because of what she
felt had been a personal slight years before. She also
prevented the appointment of Alice Roosevelt's husband,
Nick Longworth, as minister to China. At one point,
Helen was overheard telling her husband, "I could not
believe you to be serious when you mentioned that man's
name. I won't even talk about it."

After only two and a half months in the White House,
Nellie suffered a minor stroke that incapacitated her for a
year. When she had recovered enough to resume her
duties, she made up for lost time with grand parties and
twice as many social affairs as any administration before.
There were guests for dinner every night and often for
breakfast. Although musicales had been held at the
White House before, Nellie was the first to have them
after official state dinners. In 1910, she organized a lavish
affair for the debut of their daughter, Helen. The
following year, the Tafts celebrated their silver wedding
anniversary with a spectacular party on the White House
lawn to which six thousand people were invited.

Some of her innovations as First Lady were ridiculed.
For appearance' sake, she would not allow bald waiters
or butlers in the dining room and insisted that all be
clean-shaven. She also replaced the White House police

guards with black servants pretentiously dressed in blue livery. A more popular and long-lasting change was the planting of the Tidal Basin area and Capitol grounds with three thousand cherry trees. The trees had been donated by the mayor of Tokyo when Nellie made known her desire for them.

Nellie would have liked to remain in the White House for a second four years, but it was not to be. An agonizing rupture had occurred in the friendship between Taft and Roosevelt. As a result of a split between Taft's more conservative policies and Roosevelt's newly formed progressive Bull Moose party, the Republicans lost to the Democratic candidate, Woodrow Wilson.

For eight years after leaving the White House, the Tafts lived in New Haven, Connecticut, where he was a professor at Yale. Nellie wrote her autobiography, *Recollections of Full Years*, which was published in 1914. In 1921, President Harding appointed William Chief Justice of the Supreme Court. This time Nellie was happy to have him accept. It is what he had wanted all along.

After William's death in 1930, Nellie remained in Washington, where she died in 1943. Her intelligence, activism, and political savvy lived on in her children. The eldest son, Robert (known as "Mr. Republican"), became prominent in politics, served in the U.S. Senate for fifteen years, and ran for president three times. The second son, Charles, was active in civic movements to help the underprivileged and served as mayor of Cincinnati. Daughter Helen, with a doctorate in history and a law degree, became, for a time, acting president of Bryn Mawr College and was active in the suffragist movement.

Ellen Louise Axson Wilson
1860–1914

"ANGEL IN THE WHITE HOUSE"
Woodrow Wilson Administration 1913–21

❖

Ellen Wilson was First Lady for less than two years but made a more lasting impression than some of her predecessors. One member of the household staff thought she was "an angel in the White House." A talented painter, who at one time had wanted to devote her life to artistic achievements, Ellen became one of the first First Ladies to act on her strong social conscience to try to improve the lives of others.

Ellen Louise Axson was born in Rome, Georgia, to a Presbyterian minister who suffered frequent nervous breakdowns and died in a mental institution in 1884. She had been earning money for her crayon portraits since

ELLEN LOUISE AXSON WILSON

she was eighteen, then a small inheritance from her father enabled her to study art for a year at the Art Students' League in New York. By then she was engaged to graduate student Woodrow Wilson. They had met when he had visited relatives in her hometown, and Woodrow was immediately smitten by the girl "with hair like burnished copper" and "splendid laughing eyes." The couple was married in 1885.

The Wilsons began married life in Bryn Mawr, Pennsylvania, where Woodrow taught history and political science. Ellen became proficient enough in German to translate German monographs for him. She also came to know her husband's need to be cosseted by women who would admire his intelligence and laugh at his jokes. Realizing that she was not enough of an audience for him, she tried to arrange it so that he was surrounded by lively people—and then not show any jealousy of his women friends. Their three daughters—Jessie, Margaret, and Eleanor—also grew up to idolize their father.

The family moved to Princeton, New Jersey, where they lived for twenty-three years. Woodrow taught and then became president of the university. He was elected governor in 1911 and U.S. president in 1920.

Just before the inauguration, Ellen had her first one-woman show in Philadelphia, which was favorably reviewed and from which twenty-four of her landscape paintings were sold. The proceeds were given to the Martha Berry School, which had been founded to educate underprivileged and mountain children; everything she made from her art was either given to this school or to another charity.

Ellen had some forebodings about living in the White House, even breaking into tears on the morning of the inaugural, but she fairly quickly made the place her own, adding books, chintz curtains, her piano and art, including the return of a painting of two nudes that the more prudish Helen Taft had removed from the mansion. She installed her work studio in a skylighted room on the third floor. However, as mistress of the executive mansion, she did not have much time for painting.

The appalling conditions of the slums (inhabited primarily by blacks and recent immigrants) in the alleys within a few blocks of the White House were brought to Ellen's attention by Washington social activist Mrs. Archibald Hopkins. Without fanfare or publicity, the First Lady went to see them for herself and was impressed—or depressed—enough to become honorary (though active) chairman of the advisory board for the housing committee of the Women's Department of the National Civic Federation. She worked with the committee to draft legislation for an "alley bill," which was introduced in Congress in February 1914. Although she had the somewhat paternalistic views of Southern women of that time on the place of blacks in society, favoring segregated facilities in government offices, the First Lady cared enough about the people to try to improve their squalid living conditions—their dilapidated shacks and the epidemics brought on by unsanitary conditions.

Ellen was also taken to visit the Home for Incurables, where she shook the hand of every patient. Her visit there and her obvious concern about conditions in the back alleys made slum improvement a fashionable topic of conversation in Washington. In lending the prestige of her position as First Lady to worthwhile causes, she set a trend that many women in the White House would follow in the future.

Ellen used the hand-woven products of the women from the mountains of poor Southern states in redecorating the White House, which helped to create an interest and market for these goods. She was named honorary president of the Southern Industrial Association and showed a public interest in their fund-raising events in the capital, including an exhibition of their quilts, rugs, and fabrics in the White House.

She took an interest, too, in what she thought were the unsanitary conditions at government agencies, especially the lack of rest rooms for the hundreds of women employees. Shortly before her death, she received a letter from the Government Printing Office thanking her for working to see that the seventeen hundred women there finally had toilets.

Being a gracious hostess was no hardship for a genteel Southern woman, but she was not known for her lively parties—even the inaugural ball had been canceled because the Wilsons thought it would be too frivolous. Serving tea in the White House gardens was one of her favorite forms of entertainment. The most interesting social events to take place in the White House were the weddings of two Wilson daughters: Jessie married Frank Sayre in the East Room before five hundred guests on November 25, 1913. Nell surprised everyone by falling for the secretary of the treasury, William G. McAdoo, a fifty-year-old widower with six children. They were married in a quiet ceremony in the smaller Blue Room on May 7, 1914.

One of the reasons for the small wedding was that Ellen was now in poor health. She had had a fall in her bedroom in March and seemed to be in frail health from that time. She was suffering from Bright's disease, a kidney disorder, from which her doctor knew she would not recover, although the president was not told it was hopeless until the last days. Hours before she died (at fifty-four), she told her husband that she could "go away more cheerfully" if she knew that the alley bill had been passed by Congress. On hearing this, the Senate passed it unanimously, and the House agreed to pass it the next day. She was told this shortly before losing consciousness. (After her death, this legislation was declared unconstitutional, and the slums are still with us.)

Her legacy as a First Lady who cared for people endures, despite the eventual failure of government to act on her plans, because of her strong but soft-spoken convictions. She once expressed them in a letter, saying, "I wonder how anyone who reaches middle age can bear it if she cannot feel, on looking back, that whatever mistakes she may have made she has on the whole lived for others and not for herself."

Edith Bolling Galt Wilson
1872–1961

"PETTICOAT GOVERNMENT"
Woodrow Wilson Administration 1913–21

❖

Several First Ladies, from Abigail Adams to Helen Taft, had been accused of being too strong an influence on their husbands, but Edith Wilson was in a class by herself. Because her husband was completely incapacitated for at least six weeks, people said she was actually taking on the full duties of the president. No one but Edith and the doctors knew exactly what was going on in the president's darkened sickroom, but it seems unlikely today that the First Lady wanted power; she just wanted what so many of them did, and still do: to protect her husband.

A proud, ninth-generation descendant of Pocahontas and John Rolfe, Edith Bolling was born in Wytheville,

EDITH BOLLING GALT WILSON

Virginia, one of nine children of Sallie White and Judge William Bolling. The family was poor, having lost its plantation near Appomattox, Virginia, in the Civil War, and her education was spotty, consisting of some home tutoring and then two years of finishing school.

While visiting a sister in Washington, D.C., Edith met Norman Galt, owner of a prosperous jewelry store. She married him in 1896. When Galt died twelve years later, she directed the store's management for two years and then sold it for a handsome sum. Childless, she took as her protégée Altrude Gordon, the teenage daughter of a friend who had died. Altrude later married Woodrow Wilson's physician, Dr. Gary Grayson. It was Dr. Grayson who first introduced the forty-three-year-old Edith to Helen Bones, cousin and companion of the recently widowed president.

Helen and Edith accidentally ran into the president and his doctor one afternoon in the White House; they had tea and the president laughed for the first time since his first wife had died seven months earlier. Within two months of meeting the tall (5 feet 9 inches), buxom, gay Widow Galt, Woodrow proposed (in April). She accepted in September, but only after a new phrase came into the American lexicon. Some of the president's advisers felt that the marriage was too hasty for the American electorate, who they hoped would be re-electing him in 1916. They warned him that if he went through with it, a certain Mrs. Peck would publish the very warm and friendly letters he had written her some years before. As rumors of these letters flew through the capital, Wilson came to be known—to the disrespectful—as Peck's Bad Boy. The men responsible for the rumor, Colonel Edward House and son-in-law McAdoo, later admitted that they had fabricated the danger to delay or prevent the marriage.

During their three-month engagement, Woodrow had begun his practice of talking over everything with Edith, and installed a direct phone line from the White House to her home. She was kept up to date on the developments of the war in Europe as well as on domestic matters, beginning what she referred to as a "partnership of thought and comradeship" and which served as her political education. They married on December 18, 1915, and the next morning he was observed clicking his heels and singing, "Oh, you beautiful doll."

During the stressful years of World War I, Edith devoted much of her energies to getting her husband to relax and exercise by playing golf. Meatless, wheatless, and all the other "less" days in American homes were also observed at the White House. The observance of gasless Sundays ended their Sunday pleasure drives. Social activities were also curtailed, as Edith spent her time serving food at the Red Cross canteen and sewing pajamas for the soldiers in hospitals. She raised $100,000 for the Red Cross by auctioning off the wool of the sheep which were brought in to clip the White House lawns, freeing the yardmen for the war effort. She also had the job of naming warships, most of which sailed off with an American Indian name because of Edith's own Indian heritage.

Woodrow never went anywhere without Edith; after the Armistice, she accompanied him to Europe, exulting in the tremendous ovations he received wherever they went. She could not understand how the European leaders could give the great man such a hard time on adopting his Fourteen Points at the Paris peace conference. Following months of dogged efforts to push through an acceptable peace treaty, Woodrow suffered what was then diagnosed as influenza but is now thought to have been a cerebral thrombosis.

He might have lived many years without a reoccurrence if things had gone his way in Congress on his return to the States, but the Republicans in the Senate, led by Henry Cabot Lodge, were balking at his plan for joining a League of Nations. Since Woodrow considered this one of the most important of the fourteen points of his peace treaty already approved in Europe, he decided to take his case to the people on a cross-country train trip.

For twenty-two days, the Wilsons traveled through the heat of middle America with little time for rest between appearances. As the days passed, Woodrow's excruciating headaches became more frequent and his insomnia worsened until one night outside of Wichita, Kansas, he asked his wife to come to him because he was so "terribly sick."

Edith convinced the heartbroken president that he could not continue and allow the people to see him as he was, the left side of his face fallen and his speech slurred and indistinct. The report given to the press was "a complete nervous breakdown" requiring rest back at the White House. Once back in Washington, a curtain was drawn between his sickroom and the public, a curtain behind which his true condition was to remain a mystery to all but his wife and doctors.

A few days after returning to the White House, Edith found her husband unconscious on the bathroom floor. His left side was by then completely paralyzed, and his condition was critical for weeks. Thus began what the press dubbed "Mrs. Wilson's Regency" and "petticoat government," but what she called her stewardship. For the remaining seventeen months of Woodrow's term—although she claimed that her role only lasted the six weeks before he recovered enough to take over—she directed the executive branch of government with the sole purpose of doing what she thought best for her husband. When she broached the subject of resignation with the doctors, she was told that removing his sense of purpose could kill him. And besides, Vice President Marshall had no ambition to rise above his number-two position.

In what must be one of the most politically naive statements ever made, Edith answered her critics by saying, "I, myself, never made a single decision regarding the disposition of public affairs. The only decision that was mine was what was important and what was not, and the *very* important decision of when to present matters to my husband." Having been his close confidante for four years, she was not in the dark as to his thoughts on many matters, but she also took the opportunity to distance him from such men as his secretary Joseph Tumulty and Colonel House, who might have been able to advise and inform him, because of her own dislike for them. She even ignored Secretary of State Lansing with the explanation, "I never liked him."

Several Republicans, including Senator Albert Fall of New Mexico, hoping to prove the president either insane or incompetent, finally arranged a sickroom meeting. With Edith by his side taking notes "so there may be no misunderstandings or misstatements made," Woodrow gathered enough strength for a successful interview. As the disappointed Fall was leaving, he took the president's hand and said, "Mr. President, I am praying for you," to which Woodrow replied, "Which way, Senator?"

Edith had what she called "a workable system" for dealing with affairs of state, which involved reading everything addressed to the president, seeking his opinion on what she considered the important questions, and then telling the official involved what the president's decision was. Democrats trying to pass his treaty in the Senate urged her to press him to accept a compromise on the League, but when she went to him and asked him to accept and "get this awful thing settled," he just replied, "Little girl, don't you desert me."

He did eventually meet with his cabinet again; he even fired Lansing for holding meetings without him while he was incapacitated. But Woodrow tired easily, his mind wandered, and he was never again completely in charge. Sadly, he had dreams of running for another term so that he could continue to push for U.S. entry into the League of Nations, but the League was doomed and so was the Democrat party when Republican Warren Harding was elected president.

When Woodrow died three years after leaving office, Edith took up the "cause" of honoring his memory, which she continued until her death in 1961 at eighty-nine. She served as a director of the Woodrow Wilson Foundation and never completely left the political arena again, supporting Democratic candidates by appearing at their functions. A year before she died, she sat behind John F. Kennedy at his inauguration.

Before marrying Woodrow, Edith had been completely unpolitical and was even opposed to women's suffrage, calling the picketing suffragettes "detestable," so it is ironic that, as First Lady, she should be the one most vehemently accused of usurping power.

Florence Kling DeWolfe Harding 1860–1924

"MOLDER OF A PRESIDENT"
Warren G. Harding Administration 1921–23

❖

In contrast to the maligned Edith Wilson, the formidable Florence Harding was more than an influence in her husband's life. "Flossie" was the sculptor, the very molder of a president. She didn't do it alone, but it wouldn't have happened without her. She took an affable, handsome, not very astute man (a man with what Woodrow Wilson called a "bungalow mind") from a small town in the Midwest and put him in the White House, where he belonged only as a visitor.

Florence was born in 1860, the daughter of Louisa and Amos Kling, a wealthy businessman from Marion, Ohio. She attended the Cincinnati Conservatory of Music until

FLORENCE KLING DEWOLFE HARDING

her mother died. Still a teenager, Flossie lived at home giving piano lessons until she could no longer stand the restrictions her domineering father imposed on her and eloped with Henry DeWolfe, the neighborhood rogue. Six months later, she had a son, and soon after that her husband deserted her.

The nineteen-year-old divorcee briefly supported herself and her child by teaching piano. Eventually her father let her back into the family home. When she was thirty, she met the handsome twenty-five-year-old publisher of the *Marion Daily Star*, Warren G. Harding. Over her father's objections again, she set out to catch this young bachelor and succeeded. This time her father did not speak to her for seven years, and would not enter her house for fifteen more.

Shortly after their marriage in 1891, Warren suffered one of his periodic "nervous breakdowns," and his wife went to fill in for him at the newspaper. She stayed for fourteen years. Her reorganization of the business side of the enterprise contributed greatly to its success. Also, with Florence in the office every day, her husband had more time to pursue his interest in politics and to speak to Republican groups. His speeches were mellifluous and florid, and until he became president, no one noticed that they were also short on ideas.

His speaking style, his handsome, full-maned head and erect carriage oiled his way to the state senate, the lieutenant governorship, and, in 1914, the U.S. Senate. Both Hardings were happy with him in the Senate; there was prestige without the danger of doing much harm. But politics moves in mysterious ways, and the GOP began to take seriously the idea of putting Warren G. Harding in the White House in 1920.

The instigator of this strange plot was Ohio's political boss Harry Daugherty, but Flossie became his willing accessory and the driving force behind the wavering resolve of the often reluctant candidate. Flossie had had some doubts herself at first, saying that being a senator's wife suited her. She had always been a superstitious woman who often consulted mediums and the stars, and she seemed to understand one message correctly when she claimed to "see but one word written over his head if they make him President and that word is Tragedy." Unfortunately, she ignored that warning when she became blinded by the alluring light of living in the White House.

As the first discouraging nomination returns came in, Warren, or Wurr'n as she pronounced it, tried to phone Daugherty and withdraw his name, but from across the room Flossie spotted him. She scurried over, took the receiver, and told Daugherty they were in to stay and hung up. President-maker Daugherty liked to boast that the two of them "backed [Warren] against the wall and made him stick."

After the inauguration, the new First Lady, with great self-satisfaction, said to her husband, "Well, Warren Harding, I have got you the presidency; what are you going to do with it?" To which the hapless president replied, "May God help me, for I need it." He knew he was "a man of limited talents" and admitted to his cronies, with whom he still liked to spend his nights playing poker, that he couldn't seem to grasp the idea that he really was president. He even insisted that they not call him Mr. President or treat him any differently.

But Warren knew "the Duchess," as he called his wife, wanted to "be the drum major in every band that passes." He seemed to be somewhat afraid of her, and would check with her on important decisions. And she watched him very closely. Her understanding of political issues seemed to be better than his, and she advised him on appointments and used a heavy editorial hand on his speeches, even rewriting his inaugural address. She believed that he always did well if he took her advice but not otherwise.

First Lady Harding, saying that they were just "plain folks," reopened the mansion to visitors after the somber years of war and Wilson's illness; she liked to come downstairs and mingle with the surprised and delighted tourists. She was also a great favorite with the wounded veterans in the local hospitals, whom she would visit and invite to the White House. Upstairs in the mansion, Warren's poker parties continued with Flossie making the drinks in spite of prohibition.

There was, however, a darker side. She was possessive and jealous of Warren—and her suspicions about him and other women were usually correct. In speaking of his "girlies," Alice Roosevelt Longworth said he "put the White House closets to a whole new range of uses." Flossie was five years older than Warren (sixty in 1920) and spent a lot of time and money on daily facials and expensive clothes. She never admitted to having two grandchildren (they were never invited to the White House) and always wore a ribbon around her neck to hide the wrinkles. Never very attractive, she was considered overdressed, overcoiffed, and overrouged.

She was not an easy woman to live with; the White House housekeeper wrote some years later that Florence Harding "had a temper that was almost uncontrollable at times." She once shouted over the banister to her fleeing husband, "You are not leaving this house tonight." He walked out anyway. She also had a little red "grudge book" in which she kept a list of the people who had snubbed her, and she once told Alice Longworth that "those people were to realize that she was aware of their behavior." Because of personal animosity toward Vice President Calvin Coolidge and his attractive wife, she managed to sabotage a bill that would have given vice presidents a permanent home, snorting, "I just couldn't have people like those Coolidges living in that beautiful house."

In 1922, a chronic kidney problem flared up again and very nearly killed her. By the time she could be active again, the troubles besetting the president had become unmanageable, and she had lost control. Rumors of corruption on the part of Warren's staff and cabinet members bubbled to the surface daily, and the Hardings, both of whom were physically unwell and mentally unable to take charge of the situation, decided on a change of scene with a trip to Alaska. Bad news followed the dispirited couple as they trained across the country trying to escape the revelations of graft, extortion, and suicide in their "Ohio Gang."

On August 3, 1923, while resting in San Francisco after seeing Alaska, Harding suffered a blood clot on the brain and died. Thankfully, he didn't live to see the worst revelations of corruption, including the infamous Teapot Dome scandal, in which several of his cronies were convicted for their part in leasing government oil reserves to private companies.

As his body lay in state in the East Room redolent with flowers, the Duchess spent the night tearlessly talking to him. She was heard to say, "No one can hurt you now, Warren," but what else she said and thought will never be known. Before her own death in November 1924 she burned all of Wurr'n's and her personal papers.

Grace Anna Goodhue Coolidge
1879–1957

"NATIONAL HUGGER"
Calvin Coolidge Administration 1923–29

Author Gamaliel Bradford wrote of the Coolidges that "the man would not have been what he was without the woman, and most of all precisely because of her infinite, exquisite tact in effacing herself." Grace Coolidge's warm and vivacious personality was an essential antidote to the wooden and dour personality of her husband in the White House.

Grace, the only child of Andrew and Lemira Barrett Goodhue, was born in 1879 and raised in Burlington, Vermont. She was a handsome young woman with gray-green eyes, a full mouth, and thick wavy dark hair who was "given to blithe spontaneous laughter," accord-

GRACE ANNA GOODHUE COOLIDGE

ing to a friend. In 1902, she was graduated from the University of Vermont and left home to become a teacher at the Clarke Institute for the Deaf in North-ampton, Massachusetts.

One day she looked up from her gardening and saw a man in the neighboring house in his bedroom window, shaving in his union suit, with his hat on. This was the young attorney and aspiring-politician Calvin Coolidge. She laughed out loud at this sight, naturally. Calvin heard her and wanted to meet the person who could laugh so brightly and to explain to her that he kept his hat on while shaving to keep his hair out of his eyes. She had been teaching the deaf for three years, and Calvin expressed the hope that "maybe having taught the deaf to hear, Miss Goodhue might perhaps cause the mute to speak." They were married in 1905, but she never did have much luck getting him to talk.

They moved into half of a modest two-family house, and it remained their home, to the dismay of the aristocratic senator from Massachusetts Henry Cabot Lodge, throughout Calvin's career. Their two sons, John and Calvin Jr., were born here. When Calvin became governor of Massachusetts, he refused to move his family to Boston, but stayed in a hotel room and commuted on weekends, depriving Grace of valuable hostessing experience. This pattern continued when he became Harding's vice president in 1920. The couple could not afford to buy a house in the capital, so they set up housekeeping in the Willard Hotel with their young sons. Grace confided to friends that, as a result, she was "more proficient in setting up and operating miniature tracks and trains on the dining-room floor than in receiving and entertaining guests in the drawing room."

When President Harding died in 1923, the Coolidges were at the Plymouth, New Hampshire, farm of Calvin's father, who happened to be a notary public. Father gave son the oath of office as President of the United States. Since it was the middle of the night, sensible Calvin then took his wife and went back to bed.

The new president had very firm ideas about how a First Lady—at least his First Lady—should conduct herself. She should not dance in public or drive a car or go horseback riding or speak on politics or bob her hair or go up in a plane, even though it was Charles Lindbergh who offered her the ride. Calvin felt that she would do a better job if she did nothing new, an attitude that seemed to Grace to have the "semblance of a death notice." She responded to his edict against giving interviews with typical humor at a picnic she gave for women reporters. When they requested a speech, she raised her hands and spoke to them in the sign language she had mastered as a teacher of the deaf.

As Alice Longworth noted, the new First Lady "put no feminine finger into affairs of state," but she did remember faces and something of what was behind them and made White House guests feel welcome. With her warm, spontaneous nature, she did "the front door job" for the Coolidges. She was photographed so often hugging children that she joked that she might become known as the "National Hugger."

Being married to Silent Cal, Grace knew that "as a dinner guest there is no denying that he was unsatisfactory." The family doctor observed that "she would encourage him to talk and when he wouldn't she quickly filled in the gaps." Calvin would not or could not make small talk and was too restless to sit for long. At one White House dinner, he rose from the table early, and when she reminded him that the guests had not finished their dessert, he replied, "I have." Afterward, Grace would treat such incidents humorously and get the guests to laugh with her.

Rather than making excuses for her husband's eccentricities, Grace contributed to his reputation as a character by telling amusing stories about him, and there was much affectionate teasing between them. When she remarked that she was "a little more domestically inclined" than Calvin, he contradicted her, saying that "she has kept me running for public office ever since I married her." Once, at breakfast the morning after a dinner on the presidential yacht, at which Calvin spoke very little to the two women beside him, he asked Grace where the women were. She shot back, "Exhausted by your conversation of last evening."

Grace could laugh even when he described her pie crusts and muffins as something more suitable for road construction than eating because, as everyone knew, "she was the sunshine and the joy in his life." When she was away visiting relatives, he pounced on the mail and locked himself in his room for half an hour to read her letters.

A few months after becoming First Lady, Grace was the hostess at a White House reception for the diplomatic corps from forty-nine nations. During the social season, she gave teas in the Red Room on most Monday and Friday afternoons and liked to have musicales after dinners. She entertained the Queen of Rumania, Crown Prince Gustavus Adolphus of Sweden, a prince of Japan, Lindbergh (just after his historic flight), Will Rogers, and others. According to Colonel Starling of the Secret Service, who was present at most of the occasions, Grace was "amazingly successful as a hostess, being gracious and friendly without an air of worry or flurry."

In the summer of 1924, a tragedy occurred in the Coolidge family that took away most of their enjoyment at being in the White House. Their younger son, Calvin Jr., spending some of his school vacation in the capital, played tennis one day without socks and developed a blister on his foot. An infection resulted and spread through his leg; in those pre-penicillin times, he was dead within a few days.

Coolidge ran an austere administration, checked all the bills, and poked into the refrigerators to inspect the food being served. But he did not stint when it came to Grace's wardrobe. He loved to buy her clothes and hated to see her in the same gown twice, insisting that she wear the best and most expensive. Even when they were dining alone, he and Grace put on their most elegant clothes.

When the president announced in August 1927 that he did not "choose to run," his wife was as surprised as anyone and said she had "had no idea" of his intentions. She later wrote, with an unknown amount of irony or rationalization, that she was "rather proud of the fact that after nearly a quarter of a century of marriage my husband feels free to make his decisions without consulting me or giving me advance information concerning them."

When the Coolidges retired to Northampton, they found that they didn't have enough privacy in their two-family home, and they moved across town to a large house called The Beeches. Calvin died there in 1933.

Three years later, Grace finally got the plane ride she had wanted, and she began to travel, going to Europe with a friend. She also retained her lifelong passion for baseball, knew players personally, saved scorecards from games she went to, and kept up with her favorite team, the Boston Red Sox. She continued to work with the hearing impaired and served as a trustee and president of the board of the school where she had once taught. During World War II, she worked for the Red Cross and helped to raise money to bring refugee children to the United States.

Grace was a lively, humorous First Lady who brought a much needed animation to the Coolidge White House. She also left a lasting memento: by crocheting one square for every month of her husband's tenure, she created a spread for the Lincoln bed.

Lou Henry Hoover
1874–1944

"WORLD TRAVELER"
Herbert C. Hoover Administration 1929–33

Lou Hoover was an active, well-traveled, intelligent, unusual woman, but when she moved into the White House, she chose to hide her personality and her interests. This was an unfortunate decision, for she could have been a valuable asset to her terse, stolid husband in dealing with people in troubled times.

Born in Waterloo, Iowa, in 1874, Lou was the daughter of Dr. Charles Henry, a man who had longed for a son. Happily for both of them, Lou developed a love for nature and enjoyed fishing and camping with her father when they moved to Monterey, California. At Stanford University, she was the only girl in the geology class where she met Herbert Hoover. The taciturn senior was attracted to the tall freshman with her "whimsical mind,

LOU HENRY HOOVER

her blue eyes and a broad grinnish smile" who could leap over a fence as well as he on field trips.

After her graduation, Herbert proposed to her by telegram from Australia, and she wired back, "Yes." They were married in 1899 and spent their honeymoon on a slow boat to China.

In China, where Herbert was working as a mining consultant to the emperor, Lou traveled about with her husband, often living under primitive conditions. She learned to speak Chinese, one of five languages she eventually mastered, and began what would become one of the world's finest collections of Chinese porcelains. The Hoovers were in Tientsin when the Boxer Rebellion erupted, and Lou had to ride her bicycle close to the city walls to avoid bullets from snipers as she went to and from the hospital where she helped care for the wounded.

During their marriage, the Hoovers—and eventually their two sons, Herbert and Allen—traveled through and lived in much of the world: Australia, New Zealand, Burma, Japan, Russia, Egypt, Korea, and Canada. On one of their trips, they found a copy of a sixteenth-century work on metallurgy by Georgius Agriocola, which Lou and Herbert spent several years translating from the Latin.

At the outbreak of World War I, they were living in London, and they immediately set to work helping stranded Americans return home. Lou then took the two boys back to the U.S. herself and crossed the country giving speeches to raise funds for the relief of the starving Belgians. She returned to Europe, and for her part in establishing the American Women's Hospital in Belgium, she was awarded the Cross of Chevalier, Order of Leopold by King Albert.

Throughout her busy life, she demonstrated a desire to do something for women. She founded the women's division of the National Amateur Athletic Association, was an organizer of the women's conference on law enforcement after the Teapot Dome scandal, served as president of the Girl Scouts, and advocated the participation of women in politics even if it was only to vote. She claimed that "good women elect bad men by staying away from the polls."

A woman of many talents, who read sociology and economics for enjoyment, Lou designed the Hoovers' home in Palo Alto, California, as well as the furniture for their presidential weekend house, Rapidan, in the Blue Ridge Mountains. This camp was later donated to the Shenandoah National Park.

The Hoovers settled in Washington for eight years in 1921, while Herbert served as secretary of commerce under Harding and Coolidge. Lou soon discovered what a waste of time it was for cabinet wives to spend their afternoons driving around leaving their social cards and having "at homes," and she helped to put a stop to the old practice.

As First Lady in 1929, she became an avid historian of the White House. During her research, she discovered the whereabouts of the chairs depicted in a painting of Lincoln signing the Emancipation Proclamation and brought them back to the White House. She also worked to fill the public rooms with American art and antiques and commissioned the Signal Corps to photograph the White House furnishings for a permanent record.

In the family quarters, Lou rearranged so many things so many times that the busy moving men were convinced that everything on the entire second floor had been moved somewhere "except the grand staircase and the elevator, and we're waiting to see where they're going." She created the Palm Room from the West sitting room and filled it with climbing plants, bamboo furniture, and cages of exotic birds.

Lou believed in opening the White House to as many people as possible and entertained daily at nearly every meal, including tea. This lavish entertainment, "the best table that was ever set at the White House," was possible during a time of depression because the Hoovers could pay for it from their own considerable fortune. In 1933, however, she made another break with tradition many earlier First Ladies would have welcomed: She canceled the New Year's Day reception for thousands of hand-shakers.

Lou had definite ideas about how social events should be handled. The seven-course dinners were always served at the same time, with servants standing stiffly at attention in the dining room. The butlers, who wore black ties by day and white tails in the evening, all had to be exactly the same height, as did the footmen. The help was forbidden to talk in the pantry or to clang the silver against the china, and linguist though she was, Lou thought it more efficient to give orders in body language rather than verbally. The often confused staff would try to follow her signals—a hand to her hair announced dinner, a hand on a glass meant clear the table; if she started walking around the room, it meant the interview was at an end.

The First Lady put on no airs, wore little jewelry, and avoided high heels because they slowed her down. She was a private person who gave no interviews to reporters and failed to show the public what an interesting woman she was. Once she was accused by some Southerners of having "defiled" the White House for having invited the wife of the black congressman from Chicago, Oscar De Priest, to a tea for congressional wives.

With the Great Depression, it was natural that Herbert Hoover would be one of this country's least popular presidents. There were so many threats on his life that the Secret Service resorted to extraordinary security measures—even inside the White House. When the Hoovers walked down a hallway, the staff had to get out of sight; the linen closets were often full of maids and footmen, and the gardeners learned to hide behind bushes at the signal. Herbert worked so hard that the servants took bets on how fast he would eat before going back to his office; the record was eight minutes. Lou was left to charm the guests.

In her quiet way she also did what she could to alleviate the suffering of people and hired a secretary and two assistants to help answer her mail and send out anonymous contributions to the needy.

When World War II broke out, the Hoovers were no longer in the White House, but Lou continued to work for those in need, helping the refugees in this country and the homeless in England.

She died of a heart attack in 1944, a few months after writing a note of exaggerated modesty for her family that read, "I am a lucky woman to have had my life's trail alongside the paths of three such men and boys."

Anna Eleanor Roosevelt Roosevelt 1884–1962

"FIRST LADY OF THE WORLD"
Franklin D. Roosevelt Administration 1933–45

❖

There was once a young woman, born in 1884, who grew up in the old aristocratic society of New York City and its more exclusive environs. She conformed to her caste's attitudes toward minorities, women, marriage, and her place in the world. Yet by the time Eleanor Roosevelt died in 1962, she was known as the First Lady of the World and the champion of blacks, Jews, women, the young, the poor—virtually all who ever needed a champion.

Her father, Eliott Roosevelt, was the younger brother of Teddy. Her mother, Anna Hall, was the oldest sister in a family of beautiful women. Eleanor, their only

ANNA ELEANOR ROOSEVELT ROOSEVELT

daughter, was called "plain" by family friends and "Granny" by her mother. The child's mouth and chin kept her from ever being thought attractive, but to her father she was his "little golden hair." Unfortunately, this beloved father had a weakness for alcohol and began to spend long periods away from his family—either overcome by his problem or trying to cure it—and finally he and Anna separated. He was not with eight-year-old Eleanor when her mother died of diphtheria, but when the family did allow him to visit his daughter again, he promised that someday the two of them would have a life of their own together. She lived for that time and saved every letter he wrote over the next two years before he, too, died.

Eleanor went to live with Grandma Hall, who was temperamentally unequipped to care for a sensitive, insecure child. But her rather grim existence greatly improved when she was sent at fifteen to study in England at Mme. Souvestre's Allenwood School; Eleanor called these the three "happiest years of my life." At eighteen, she returned to the U.S. to face the ordeal of coming out in society. More congenial to her puritanical nature was the work she began to do with underprivileged children at the Rivington Street Settlement.

At about this time, the tall slender young woman was beginning to attract her distant cousin Franklin. They had always known each other, but now the handsome, dashing Harvard student, consciously or not, recognized in Eleanor the traits that would combine with his for one of this country's most successful political partnerships. By her own assessment, she then had "painfully high ideals and a tremendous sense of duty . . . entirely unrelieved by any sense of humor or any appreciation of the weakness of human nature."

In 1905, Eleanor's uncle, President Theodore Roosevelt, gave her in marriage to Franklin, and into the controlling hands of her mother-in-law, Sara. Sara took charge of the young couple's housing (their adjoining New York town houses opened into each other), servants, and, eventually, their five children.

Franklin's determination to emulate Teddy's political career began with service in the New York State senate and, during World War I, as assistant secretary of the navy. The moves to Albany and Washington helped Eleanor escape Sara's clutches and also exposed her to the world outside privileged New York society. The war gave her the excuse to suspend tiresome social calls, and she busied herself working for the Red Cross, knitting, collecting funds, and serving food in Union Station. Her own austerity measures got an unintended laugh when she was quoted as saying, "Making ten servants help me do my saving has not only been possible but highly profitable."

If World War I was a catalyst for Eleanor's social awareness, another event was more traumatizing. She discovered her husband was having an affair with her social secretary, Lucy Mercer. Writing of it years later, Eleanor said that "the bottom dropped out of my own particular world" and that she "really grew up that year." For family, financial, and especially political reasons, there was no divorce, but the marriage was forever altered by Eleanor's realization that now, with the marital trust shattered, she had better make a life for herself. She learned typing, became a partner in a small furniture-manufacturing company, and taught in a girls' school in New York.

Another catalyst in her life was a rumpled little Albany reporter named Louis Howe, who joked that his face was "one of the four ugliest" in the state but who also happened to be politically brilliant. He saw a future president in Franklin as well as Eleanor's potential and her need to be involved, so he became her political mentor and, eventually, her dear friend. Howe encouraged her to use her qualities of warmth and sincerity in dealing with people, especially reporters, and built up her self-esteem by conferring with her on political matters. Their partnership marked the beginning of Eleanor's role as liaison between her husband and the rest of the world.

Then, in 1921, Franklin was stricken with polio and became permanently crippled, able to stand only with heavy braces on his legs. His mother was determined to have him live an invalid's life at their home in Hyde Park, New York, where she could look after him, but Eleanor stood up to Sara and insisted that he must continue to be involved in political life. If she had not done so, Eleanor knew that she would have become "a completely colorless echo of my husband and mother-in-law" and "might have stayed a weak character forever."

With the encouragement of Franklin and Louis Howe, Eleanor became involved in the women's division of the Democratic party, the Women's Trade Union, and the League of Women Voters and kept the Roosevelt name before the public until 1928, when her husband was elected governor of New York. She often filled in for him at political gatherings and learned how to make a thorough inspection of state institutions and report back to him.

With F.D.R.'s election to the presidency in 1932, Eleanor prepared for what she feared would be her "captivity" in the White House, but, of course, that was not to be. Shortly after the inauguration, she began to break the rules. She became the first president's wife to hold press conferences of her own. Delightedly, the few women reporters in the White House press corps called her "God's gift to newspaperwomen."

She also refused to be hampered by the Secret Service following her around. When the "Bonus Army" veterans returned to Washington, Eleanor went alone to visit them. They eventually dispersed peacefully, grateful, as one old-timer remarked, that though "Hoover sent the army, Roosevelt sent his wife."

The country was in the depths of a terrible depression when the Roosevelts entered the White House, and Eleanor threw herself into trying to alleviate the suffering. One of her pet projects was Arthurdale, a brand-new community to be established for the distressed families of Appalachia. Politically, financially, personally—Eleanor involved herself with all the planning details. Even so, it was not a complete success, and she learned some of the limitations of a First Lady's power.

"I could not help the various things in which I am interested if I did not earn the money which makes it possible." This was how Eleanor explained her unprecedented career as a First Lady who was also a paid speaker and writer. Sponsors were anxious to pay for her radio talks, and she contracted to do two lecture tours a year for $1,000 a lecture on one of five topics: Relationship of the Individual to the Community; Problems of Youth; The Mail of a President's Wife; Peace; A Typical Day at the White House. Starting in 1936, she wrote, no matter what else was happening, a syndicated daily newspaper column entitled "My Day."

Her influence in Washington was enormous but subtle. No one knew exactly how much of what she said reflected the president's ideas, and that was the way he wanted it. She was less devious than he; when a reporter asked her how it was that her column so often reflected his thoughts, Eleanor answered, "You don't just sit at meals and look at each other." On the contrary, inviting people for a meal was one of Eleanor's favorite means of allowing those with views she thought Franklin should hear to have his attention.

The amount of mail she received daily was enormous, and she would often forward the writers' requests to the appropriate government agency with her own notations, such as, "Find out about this letter. You know what it's all about." Only occasionally was she forced to invoke Franklin's power with the words, "The President has asked me. . . ."

The ceremonial demands on a First Lady were, as she had expected, "rather tiring," but she came to realize how important she was to visitors as "a symbol which tied the people . . . to their government." Eleanor was a warm and thoughtful hostess, but she could never summon up much enthusiasm for the details of menu planning. She shocked many, including her mother-in-law, when she served hot dogs to the visiting King George VI and Queen Elizabeth of England at a picnic. Franklin was once driven to write his wife a note bemoaning the monotony of his meals, saying, "I'm getting to the point where my stomach positively rebels and this does not help my relations with foreign powers. I bit two of them yesterday."

Eleanor had grown from a young woman opposed to women's suffrage to become a strong believer that "the understanding heart of women" should be involved in trying to solve the problems of the Thirties and in working for peace. Her book, *It's Up to the Women*, published soon after she became First Lady, urged women to take part in the necessary social changes as well as politics. She also used her influence when she could to try to have qualified women appointed to government positions.

As a child, Eleanor had heard black people spoken of as "darkies," and she used the term herself in her autobiography, but as First Lady she showed her awareness that the Negro problem was a "vast issue." Walter White, head of the NAACP, found that he could always reach her with his concerns about blacks being included in New Deal programs and about proposed antilynching laws. Eleanor became his conduit to the president. In what was probably her most dramatic show of support for black rights, she resigned from the DAR when that organization refused to allow Marian Anderson to sing in Constitution Hall. The concert later took place outdoors at the Lincoln Memorial before 75,000 people.

The Fascist threat in Europe and Asia overcame Eleanor's longing for peace, and when the U.S. entered the war, she put her considerable energies into helping the enlisted men. She sent so many requests for assistance to General George Marshall's office that he assigned two staff members just to deal with them. She urged the Red Cross and U.S.O. to open a canteen in Union Station, then helped usurp a State Department reception room where servicemen passing through the capital could sleep.

In 1942, F.D.R. sent her to England to demonstrate American support and try to iron out problems in relations between the American and English soldiers. Prime Minister Winston Churchill, not one of Eleanor's favorite people because of his imperialistic attitude, thought her visit such a success that he wrote her a note saying, "You certainly have left golden footprints behind you."

A year later, slogging through the South Pacific islands, she visited about 400,000 G.I.s. Admiral Halsey reported that, in the hospitals, "she went into every ward, stopped at every bed and spoke to every patient . . . she walked for miles and she saw patients who were grievously and gruesomely wounded. But I marveled most at their expressions as she leaned over them. It was a sight I will never forget."

Back in the capital, Eleanor was as busy as ever on the day she learned that Franklin had died, April 12, 1945, in Warm Springs, Georgia. When Harry Truman was given the news, the stunned vice president asked Eleanor what he could do for her. She turned the question away from herself, asking, "Is there anything *we* can do for *you?* For you are the one in trouble now."

She was sure that for her "the story is over," but she lived for fifteen more years and proved that her effectiveness was not dependent on her husband. In 1946, she was appointed by President Truman as a delegate to the organizational meeting in London for the formation of the United Nations General Assembly. She was chairman of the U.N. commission that worked for two years to draft a declaration of human rights, which was overwhelmingly adopted by the General Assembly. She traveled, she supported the Democratic party, she even had her own television discussion show. She died in 1962 at seventy-eight. One of the last checks she wrote was her annual ten-dollar birthday gift to one of her godchildren—the daughter of a hitchhiker she had picked up and fed during the depression.

Eleanor Roosevelt was like no other First Lady before or since. Of course, her tenure was four years longer than anyone else's, but more important, she had what she called "this horrible sense of obligation which was bred in me, I couldn't help it." Nor could she help being her husband's sometimes nagging conscience. He had used her as his eyes and ears, and she reported to him what had to be done whether he wanted to hear it or not. Whenever it was suggested that she run for public office, Eleanor declined, knowing that she could not have been as effective if she had to worry about politics. The Roosevelts were probably the best combination for the country at the time of a great depression and a world war. It was a partnership between a president who had the power but had to consider political repercussions and a First Lady who had a heart and didn't have to answer to the electorate.

Elizabeth "Bess" Wallace Truman 1885–1982

"THE BOSS"
Harry S. Truman Administration 1945–53

❖

Elizabeth "Bess" Truman was called the Boss by her adoring husband, but she was never really that. No one could boss Harry Truman around, anyway. But her influence was constant and strong; Harry claimed she was a "full partner in all my transactions—politically and otherwise." He depended on her presence as a confidante, and he listened to her advice. Private may be the word to describe Bess Truman; she allowed very little of her personality or opinions to be seen in public, although she had plenty of both.

What the country saw in photos of the First Lady was a somewhat overweight, plainly dressed, gray-haired

ELIZABETH "BESS" WALLACE TRUMAN

woman in her sixties. What the president saw was the "blue-eyed golden-haired girl" he had loved since he was seven years old and she was six, when they were in school together in Independence, Missouri.

Elizabeth Wallace's family was prominent in town, and her childhood was filled with the things she loved: tennis (she was the best player in Independence), basketball, close friends, and long walks. When she was eighteen, tragedy changed her life; her father, David Wallace, committed suicide after years of financial reversals and bouts with alcoholism. Mrs. Wallace took Bess and her three brothers to live in her parents' home and became increasingly reclusive and dependent on her children. This family home was passed to Mrs. Wallace when her parents died, and it was the same house to which the Trumans retired and where they died.

To keep her sons close, Bess's mother had two homes built in the back of her property for the older sons when they married. Bess's own sense of responsibility led eventually to bringing her mother to live in the White House, where the elderly woman felt free to criticize the president on such issues as the firing of General Douglas MacArthur.

Bess Wallace was twenty-five years old before she began to see Harry's potential, and she was thirty-four before they were married in 1919. Harry had old-fashioned notions about marriage. Before he would even consider marriage, he intended to be certain that he could support a wife; he also wanted to have his military obligation behind him.

Harry's wartime connections started him in politics, and fifteen years after their marriage he was elected to the United States Senate. That campaign confirmed the new senator's wife in her view that politics was a dirty game and that "a woman's place in public is to sit beside her husband, be silent, and be sure her hat is on straight." Her place in private was a different matter.

Senator Truman took the then not unusual step of putting his wife on the office payroll as secretary and researcher. Of her $2,400 salary, he once said, "She earns every cent of it. I never make a speech without going over it with her, and I never make any decision unless she is in on it." Bess enjoyed life in the capital as the senator's wife, but what she considered a great misfortune was about to befall her; Harry was being touted as the vice presidential candidate.

In ordinary times, being the wife of the vice president might have appealed to Bess; it was certainly a life out of the public eye. But in 1944, it was obvious to everyone in Washington that, with his declining health, President Roosevelt might very well not live to complete his fourth term in office. Then Bess would be where she least wanted to be, in the White House. She had seen how hard the press was on the president's family, and she didn't want that for her only child, Margaret. She had also seen what the job had done to Roosevelt's health, and she didn't want that for her husband. And she had seen how accessible, busy, and outspoken Eleanor Roosevelt had been, and she didn't want that for herself.

Less than three months after Harry took the oath of office as vice president, he took one as president. And Bess was the reluctant First Lady. She was, however, determined to do the job her own way, in spite of the example of the hyperactivity of Eleanor Roosevelt's twelve years. She canceled the weekly press conferences to which the female reporters had become accustomed, announcing, "I am not the one who is elected. I have nothing to say to the public." When reporters put questions to her in writing, the First Lady's responses were terse. To one series of queries about her marriage, reception, minister, honeymoon, dress, etc., Bess sent back the reply, "June 28, 1919."

She also tried to keep the life of the family as normal as possible. She read to her mother and played Ping-Pong with Margaret. She was happiest when her bridge club from Independence came to visit. The White House staff developed a great affection for the Trumans (calling them the Three Musketeers because of their closeness) because of the considerate way the first family treated them. The First Lady would send the maids home on Sunday afternoon, saying she could turn down the beds "perfectly well by myself." The president introduced visiting dignitaries to any member of the staff who happened to wander through, whether butler, cook, or housekeeper. For a while, Bess and Margaret insisted on driving their own cars around town, until it became too difficult for the Secret Service to keep track of them.

Bess's primary concern was the president's physical and emotional health during some very trying times for him and the country—the decision to drop the A-bomb, the commitment of troops to Korea, the firing of General MacArthur, the airlift of the Berlin blockade. Although Harry insisted he had made the decision to attack Hiroshima and Nagasaki entirely on his own, he had discussed it with Bess, his sounding board on many policy matters. Most evenings, the Trumans would spend two hours in his study going over speeches and policies.

The First Lady viewed politics with so much detachment and disdain that she often could spot a falsity in a person with whom her husband was dealing, and she had a good sense of what the American people were thinking. She was a calming presence, tempering Harry's tendency to shoot from the hip and, almost always, keeping him from cussing in public.

Bess once said that what a First Lady needed was "good health and a well-developed sense of humor." She needed both in 1948. In that year, both the infrastructure of the White House and the election campaign of Harry Truman were in imminent danger of collapse. A whistle-stop tour by all three Trumans helped to convince voters that Harry deserved four more years and made fools of most of the pollsters and columnists of the day.

Repairing the White House took a little longer than being elected; the mansion had reached a state of irreversible structural decay. The president's bathtub was sinking into the floor and a leg of Margaret's piano poked right through the ceiling of the family dining room below. A congressional commission found that the walls of the old mansion were crumbling and the ceilings were cracking. W. E. Reynolds, commissioner of public buildings, said the second floor remained in place "purely from habit." (Only the outer walls of the mansion could be saved, and they had to be reinforced with steel.) During the extensive renovations, the first family moved across the street to government-owned Blair House, normally used for presidential guests.

Entertaining in Blair House was difficult because of its small size; only eighteen could be accommodated for dinner and 250 for tea. This meant doing things several times so that everyone would have a turn. During the Korean War, the First Lady would often entertain a hundred wounded soldiers at a time at afternoon parties.

In November 1950, an assassination attempt was made on the president by two Puerto Rican nationalists. One guard at Blair House was killed and another wounded. Bess now had another reason for not wanting Harry to run again in 1952.

By the spring of 1952, the Trumans were back in the magnificently renovated White House, catching up on their entertaining with state dinners, receptions, and luncheons. One of the First Lady's favorite visitors was Queen Juliana of the Netherlands.

The grand functions and guests never did go to Bess's head, and when her husband announced that he would not be a candidate for reelection, she looked, as one friend noted, "the way you do when you draw four aces." They retired to Independence where they lived quietly, working on his memoirs and setting up the Truman Library. Their daughter, Margaret, married to Clifton Daniel, often brought her four sons to visit and wrote biographies of both her parents.

Harry died in 1972 and Bess ten years later. Both are buried in the library courtyard, and by Harry's order her tombstone reads "First Lady, the United States of America, April 12, 1945–January 20, 1953."

Mary "Mamie" Geneva Doud Eisenhower 1896–1979

"FIRST LADY IN PINK"
Dwight D. Eisenhower Administration 1953–61

Mamie Eisenhower had no special projects, gave no interviews, did not speak in public, and had very little influence with her husband. She did not entertain much as First Lady, especially after her husband's 1956 heart attack. A meticulous housekeeper, she claimed that she never wanted to be anything but a wife, mother, and grandmother. She wore full, flouncy clothes, much of it in shades of her favorite color, pink; had little fringed bangs across her forehead; and was known to the world by a nickname evocative of childhood games played in the backyard. She was very popular with and admired

MARY ''MAMIE'' DOUD EISENHOWER

by the women of her time—the 1950s—as no First Lady to come after her could be with those characteristics.

Mary Geneva Doud, born in 1896 to a wealthy Iowa couple (later transported to Colorado), had little formal education. Her family traveled a great deal, and she met young Lieutenant Dwight Eisenhower on a visit to Fort Sam Houston near San Antonio, Texas. He was "the spiffiest looking man" she had ever talked to, and he thought she was "a vivacious and attractive girl, smaller than average, saucy in the look about her face." They were married nine months later (1916), just before her twentieth birthday.

As an army wife, Mamie grew accustomed to packing up and moving her family from place to place; the Eisenhowers had twenty-seven homes in thirty-eight years, ranging from Panama to Paris. The reality of a soldier's life really hit home on December 7, 1941, when Pearl Harbor was attacked. For Mamie, it was "the most terrible night of my life," second in suffering only to the time of the death of their first son in 1921. When Ike was serving as general in Europe and unable to confide his plans to her, Mamie had to rely on reports in the papers and on the radio. When a reporter breathlessly phoned her on D-day to ask what she thought of the invasion, she had to ask, "What invasion?"

Neither of the Eisenhowers had been very politically inclined before the 1950s; he wasn't sure what party he belonged to and she had never voted. But after the war, both the Democrats and the Republicans sought the war hero as a sure thing to head their ticket. The GOP won him—and the White House—for eight years.

The new First Lady had rheumatic heart problems and suffered from Ménières disease, an inner ear problem that causes dizziness. As a result, she sometimes stumbled, which may have led to the rumors of her being an alcoholic. She was also afflicted with headaches, asthma, and claustrophobia. Because of these illnesses, Mamie often spent her days in bed, where she did her paperwork on a small standup table while propped up against her pillows. If there was an important dinner or reception scheduled for the evening, she would prepare for it by resting all day. She once prescribed "a day a week in bed" for every woman over fifty.

Mamie seemed to look on moving into the White House with some dread—she broke into tears as Ike received the oath of office in 1953—because she had been hoping that they could finally settle down in a home of their own. So she took out all her frustrated homebody feelings on the White House. She used pink so much in her redecorating—tableclothes, candles, flowers—and dresses that it was no longer called just pink, it became "Mamie pink." She made surprise "white-glove" inspections and did not like to see footprints on the thick carpets. People learned to walk around the edge of the room so that the servants would not have to run in and brush up the pile again.

State dinners were always white tie and inspired more by pomp than by spontaneity. Everyone's entrance was timed and their position in the reception line carefully mapped out. The table in the State Dining Room was set up in an E-shape with the Eisenhowers sitting at the head on their thronelike mahogany chairs. A general's wife becomes accustomed to having aides tend to her wishes, and as First Lady, Mamie knew how she wanted things done. "When I go out," she ordered, "I am to be escorted to the diplomatic entrance by an usher. And when I return, I am to be met at the door and escorted upstairs."

The Eisenhowers did not go out much in the evening, preferring to stay in and eat dinner in front of the television or play cards with old friends. During Ike's second term, they did not have the receptions usually held during the social season, and whenever she could, Mamie gave state luncheons instead of dinners. She tried to preserve their privacy by putting state visitors across the street in Blair House rather than have them stay in the rooms usually reserved for guests on the second floor of the White House.

Mamie restored the Easter Egg Roll on the White House lawn, which had been halted during the war, to the children of Washington. She was fond of children and looked forward to visits of her only son, John, and his family. In 1968, her grandson, David, married Julie Nixon, daughter of Ike's vice president.

Although Ike thought his wife was "a very shrewd observer," she preferred not to discuss politics and did not try to influence him. "When Ike came home, he came home," she insisted. She once claimed that she only went to his White House office four times and "was invited each time."

Ike felt that "Mamie's biggest contribution was to make the White House liveable, comfortable and meaningful for the people who came in. . . . She exuded hospitality . . . as one of her functions . . . no matter how tired she was."

She and Ike retired to their farm in Gettysburg,

Pennsylvania, where he died in 1969. Mamie didn't travel much, although she did attend the dedications of the supercarrier *Dwight D. Eisenhower* and Eisenhower Hall at West Point. She continued to support her charitable causes and took a personal interest in Eisenhower College at Seneca Falls, New York. "I sold my Chrysler," she said, "to raise money for the college. And I wrote an article for *Reader's Digest* for the same reason."

Mamie died in November 1979 and is buried beside Ike in the chapel of the Eisenhower Library in Abilene, Kansas.

Jacqueline Lee Bouvier Kennedy Onassis
1929–

"WHITE HOUSE RESTORER"
John F. Kennedy Administration 1961–63

❖

The Kennedy White House years shine in the imaginations of many Americans as a kind of magical time, like that of the mythical kingdom of King Arthur's Camelot, and Jacqueline Kennedy was the queen. But the Camelot lasted for only a thousand days, ending tragically when John Kennedy was assassinated in Dallas, Texas. The image of his black-veiled widow, leading the funeral procession from the White House to St. Matthew's Cathedral, behind the coffin and the riderless horse, stands out in the nation's memory.

Jacqueline was born in 1929. Her parents, John "Blackie" and Janet Bouvier, were handsome, wealthy

JACQUELINE BOUVIER KENNEDY ONASSIS

people who lived and raised their two daughters in a world of culture, sophistication, and travel. When her mother divorced Bouvier and married Hugh Auchincloss, their life-style remained the same but the center of it moved from New York to Newport, Rhode Island, and Virginia.

Jacqueline attended Miss Chapin's, the exclusive girls' school in New York, and Miss Porter's, the equally exclusive boarding school in Connecticut. After being named Debutante of the Year at seventeen, she entered Vassar College, stayed for two years, then studied at the Sorbonne in Paris for a year. She completed college at George Washington University in Washington, D.C.

Jacqueline then worked for the Washington *Times Herald* as an "inquiring camera." She would prowl through the city with her hefty camera and ask questions of passersby (including Pat Nixon), then publish their answers under their photos. It was not a demanding job, but it might have led to something better in journalism if not for the fact that she had met John Kennedy at the home of mutual friends. She became engaged to the newly elected senator from Massachusetts, and they were married on September 12, 1953, in Newport with a reception for hundreds of friends and politicians.

A little more than seven years later, they were living in the White House. At thirty-one, Jacqueline Kennedy was the third youngest First Lady and one of the loveliest, with dark hair, wide-set eyes, and a cheeky smile. She was also the mother of three-year-old Caroline and an infant son, John. Not being a political animal herself, and feeling threatened by her loss of anonymity, one of her greatest desires was to protect herself and her children from the public eye. She wished to give no interviews, press conferences, or photo sessions and maintained that her "press relations will be minimum information given with maximum politeness." Privately, she called the women reporters "harpies" or witches. In an effort to calm the clamor from the press, she learned to orchestrate some of her family's publicity by periodically distributing photos of the children taken by her favorite photographers.

She refused to play the good political wife and would not attend such events as luncheons and teas for congressional wives, citing her need to spend time with the children or claiming she was overtired. Those who made excuses for her—often the president or the vice president's wife—were frequently embarrassed later by published photos of the First Lady doing what she had preferred to do, such as water skiing or attending an art exhibit. She often spent three or four days a week away from the White House at the couple's rented estate in Middleburg, Virginia.

Recovering from the birth of her son in November 1960 meant that the new First Lady started her White House activities slowly, but when she had regained her strength, her first concern was to do something about what she considered the cold, drab mansion with its "Statler" furnishings. She studied files from the Library of Congress about the White House and arranged to update them by having all the property stored in warehouses rephotographed and recatalogued.

Her aim was not to merely redecorate but to restore the mansion, feeling that "everything in the White House must have a reason for being there." (Other First

Ladies, including Grace Coolidge and Bess Truman, had also wanted to do something like this, but the funds and interest were not available at the time.) To assist in the acquisition of the antiques and artwork she thought historically important, the Fine Arts Commission for the White House was established in 1961. And to help finance this refurbishing as well as to let the tourists know what they were looking at, the First Lady arranged for a booklet, *The White House: An Historic Guide*, to be published and sold at the entrance to the mansion. She insisted that it be scholarly and not talk down to people and personally supervised all aspects of the project.

In the time it might take for most of us to redo one room, the White House was repainted, recurtained, and furnished with museum-quality pieces. A congressional bill was passed to forbid White House occupants from removing anything from the mansion. No longer would it be possible to have a sale such as President Chester Arthur held in 1882, when he sold twenty-four wagon loads of furnishings to make room for his own redecorations.

When the state rooms were as she thought they should be, Jacqueline invited the American people in to see them, giving a personally guided tour on national television in February 1962. Millions watched the First Lady in her two-piece red dress as she explained in her whispery little girl's voice the historical significance of the additions and changes in the White House.

Many people would have committed at least one cardinal sin for an invitation to the Kennedys' White House, and not just because of the new French chef, but because of the changes the First Lady was making in entertaining. Everything was more relaxed, with elegance and glamour replacing stiffness and formality. The long, tortuous reception lines were dropped (except for state dinners) in favor of a more casual mingling of the Kennedys with their guests. The more comfortable black tie was substituted for white tie. Cocktails were served before dinner. Dining hours were shortened by serving fewer courses. Conversation flowed more easily around the small (for eight to ten people) tables in place of the large U- or E-shaped tables used in previous administrations. Even the flower arrangements were more informal than the usual stilted bouquets.

Jacqueline hated theme parties but always tried to have some meaningful entertainment for her foreign dignitary guests. There was ballet for Emperor Haile Selassie of Ethiopia, who enjoyed dance; cellist Pablo Casals, who lived in Puerto Rico, played in the White House for the first time in sixty years when the Puerto Rican governor Luis Muñoz-Márin and his wife were guests; the New York City Center cast of *Brigadoon* performed for Morocco's King Hassan; and there was an Elizabethan evening for the Grand Duchess Charlotte of Luxembourg that included Basil Rathbone reciting a passage from Shakespeare.

In 1961, Pakistan president Muhammad Ayub Khan visited the U.S. and was given a state dinner at Mount Vernon, George Washington's plantation home overlooking the Potomac. This sounds like a pleasant way to spend a summer evening, but imagine the logistics involved in making sure that everything is done exactly right for such an important affair. First, the weather had to cooperate and alternative plans had to be ready in case it didn't. Then, 150 guests had to be ferried up the river, where they were met by marines lining the road up which the guests were driven in limousines to the mansion. Of course, arrangements for the food had to be made, tents erected, insects discouraged, acoustics for the National Symphony Orchestra perfected, portable lavatories discreetly hidden, and the perfect decorations displayed. The details were worked out, the evening went beautifully, and a hostess's reputation was made.

There were many stellar evenings. The after-dinner entertainment for French minister André Malraux was a concert by violinist Isaac Stern with cellist Leonard Rose and pianist Eugene Istomin. All living recipients of the Nobel Prize in the Western Hemisphere heard the president toast them at dinner with the words, "I think this is the most extraordinary collection of talent, of human knowledge, ever gathered at the White House, with the possible exception of when Thomas Jefferson dined alone." The American creative and intellectual community felt truly appreciated by the government during those years.

Jacqueline became a political asset on trips abroad and was called the "Number One Lady Goodwill Ambassador" because of the great enthusiasm she aroused. Her fluency in French, her preference for French designers and art, as well as her beauty made her a favorite in France, especially with President Charles DeGaulle. Jack, awed by the enthusiasm of the Parisians screaming for "Jacquii," introduced himself as "the man who accompanied Jacqueline Kennedy to Paris." She was just as popular in Canada, South America, India, and Pakistan.

The American fashion industry and hair stylists were enormously influenced by the First Lady's clothes and bouffant hairdo. Hollywood designer Edith Head considered her the "greatest single influence in history" on fashion. Jacqueline lookalikes—in simple, short dresses, white gloves, and pillbox hats with their hair puffed out from the sides and up from the top of their heads—popped up all over the country with varying degrees of success. What these imitators didn't realize was the amount of work required for such sartorial splendor. Because such attention was paid to Jackie, extensive planning was necessary when packing for a trip to ensure that no outfit was seen more than once, and since the First Lady often had to change outfits three or four times a day, an enormous amount of luggage was needed. Jacqueline's personal maid kept a ledger book listing all clothing and the proper accessories.

Jacqueline's interest in clothes, her high-toned entertainment, her proclivity for talking to men rather than women, her barely concealed disdain for reporters, and her cossetting of intellectuals were criticized by those who felt that the mood at the White House was not quite right for a democracy, and that the First Lady was behaving a bit too queenly.

Sympathy rebounded, however, when, in August 1963, her third child, a son, was born prematurely and died two days later. In the closeness this created between the bereaved parents, Jacqueline agreed to make a political trip to Texas with Jack in November. As they rode through Dallas in an open convertible, three shots fired from a building on the route mortally wounded the president. Jacqueline screamed, "My G—, they've killed

Jack. They've killed my husband," then cradled his shattered head in her lap as they raced to the hospital where he died. Hours later, she stood stunned, still in her blood-stained suit, with Lyndon Johnson as he took the oath of office aboard Air Force One.

She and her children moved to New York in search of privacy, but she remained in the limelight with all "the stares and pointing, and . . . the strangest stories," including speculation about her remarrying. Five years after John Kennedy's death, Jackie did remarry—to the enormously wealthy, sixty-two-year-old Greek shipping magnate Aristotle Onassis on the island of Skorpios. The interest in Jackie O., as the press took to calling her, did not wane, although now it was mostly concerned with her spending sprees, her traveling, and the developing problems of her marriage. When Onassis died in 1975 in a Paris hospital, his wife was at home in New York.

When the furor over her multimillion-dollar financial settlement as Onassis's widow had died down, life went on a little more quietly for Jacqueline. She began to work as an editor with a New York publisher and continued to devote herself to her children, believing that "if you fail with your children then I don't think that anything else in life could ever really matter very much."

Claudia "Lady Bird" Alta Taylor Johnson 1912–

"SHE PLANTED A TREE"
Lyndon B. Johnson Administration 1963–69

❖

Lady Bird Johnson once summed up her role as the president's wife thusly: "A First Lady should be a showman and a salesman, a clotheshorse and a publicity sounding board, with a good heart and a real interest in the folks in 'Rising Star' and 'Rosebud,' as well as Newport and whatever the other fancy places are. . . . Well, the last—real interest—I do have."

She came to the White House as the result of the Kennedy assassination rather than an election, but she rose to the challenge of being First Lady and filled that nebulous position as few women have done since Eleanor Roosevelt. Those who knew her were not surprised. A

CLAUDIA "LADY BIRD" TAYLOR JOHNSON

determined, intelligent woman married to the volcanic Lyndon Johnson for thirty years would have had to know something about adapting.

Claudia Alta Taylor was born in 1912 near the tiny town of Karnack, Texas, to Thomas Jefferson Taylor, one of the area's most wealthy men, and ethereal, slightly eccentric Minnie, who died when Claudia was just five years old. She was a shy young girl whose timidity was surely not helped by having to live with the nickname "Lady Bird," given to her by a family nurse who exclaimed that the baby, Claudia, was "as purty as a Lady Bird."

Attending the University of Texas in Austin brought her out of her shell somewhat and awakened the desire to lead an exciting life. After receiving her B.A. degree in 1933, she stayed on for another year to obtain a degree in journalism. A newspaperwoman's life seemed to her to have great potential for adventure, but before she could discover what her own adventure might be, she was caught up in the whirlwind career of Lyndon Johnson.

Lady Bird did not take full advantage of her petite, dark-eyed, brunette good looks. Her nose was longer than average, leading her to remark later in life that if she had known she would be in the White House, she would have changed her name and her nose. But Lyndon was smitten with her; on their first date, a breakfast, he proposed. She, naturally, was hesitant but had "a queer sort of moth-and-the-flame feeling about what a remarkable man he was." Her father liked Lyndon and told her that this time she had "brought home a man" instead of a boy, and Lyndon bombarded her with letters and phone calls from Washington, where he was then secretary to

Texas congressman Richard M. Kleberg. Two months later, Lady Bird was convinced—or overwhelmed—and they were married.

Once in their little apartment in the capital, Lady Bird discovered she had a lot to learn. She knew nothing about the kitchen, and had to learn to cook in order to feed all the people Lyndon would bring home at the last minute. He also had very definite ideas about how she should wear her hair and makeup and how she should dress—in bright colors and high heels instead of her comfortable, but to him "muley-lookin', " flats.

In 1937, she borrowed $10,000 on her future inheritance to finance Lyndon's successful campaign for Congress, and they were on their way. It was while Congressman Johnson was serving in the South Pacific for seven months in 1942 that his wife discovered she had a real interest in and aptitude for politics. She ran his congressional office with the same thoroughness and determination to learn that she did everything else, and after a few months felt that "if it was ever necessary, I could make my own living." Lyndon admitted later that "the tenth district would happily have elected her over me, if she had run."

Her business acumen (and to some extent, her journalistic ability) was brought out in 1942, when she took the rest of her inheritance from her mother and bought radio station KTBC in Texas. She spent seven months in Austin turning around a losing business.

During the years with Lyndon as congressman, senator, and vice president, Lady Bird found that she could do many things she didn't like to do, such as flying and giving speeches and leaving her two young daughters,

Lynda Bird and Luci Baines, while she traveled with her demanding husband. One part of being a politician's wife she did like was meeting "the people behind the statistics," and she went into the White House with many friends behind her—some of them in spite of her husband.

So when she said that becoming First Lady was like being "suddenly on stage for a part I never rehearsed," it was not quite accurate. She entered the White House with the realization that there was a time limitation and that it "will never happen again, and you can drum up the energy from somewhere within you to go more, do more, learn more." Lady Bird took the job of First Lady very seriously. She studied her guest lists to learn something about the people visiting the mansion, and before entertaining diplomats and heads of state, spent time studying maps and briefing papers.

Because of her training, Lady Bird was naturally sympathetic to the needs of the nearly eighty-five reporters who covered her activities. She appointed Liz Carpenter, a reporter, to be her press secretary—previous First Ladies had assigned public relations types to this job. It was Liz who described her friend and boss as having "a touch of velvet, with the stamina of steel."

Lady Bird felt that as a public figure, her job was "to help my husband do his job" and to carry out his plans and purposes. She once said that if she left "any footprints in the sands of time, it will be because he has been able to achieve something." In this too humble way, she became involved in those projects that most interested her—supporting the War on Poverty and the Headstart Program, continuing Jacqueline Kennedy's work on restoring the White House, encouraging people to discover America, and, most important, working for the beautification of the capital and the nation. "She Planted a Tree" was the epitaph she wanted.

In President Johnson's State of the Union Address in January 1965, he emphasized preserving America's beauty, "the green legacy for tomorrow," and Lady Bird knew that she had found her cause. She hated it when people referred to beautification as her gimmick, because she really did feel strongly that making public areas attractive improved the quality of people's lives. And the term "beautification" bothered her; she felt it did not encompass all that her project meant.

She wanted to "make a showcase of beauty on the Mall," but there was more to it than that. She and her committees wanted to interest volunteers from neighborhoods and businesses in improving the scruffy little triangles and squares that abound in the capital and to persuade the people living in the areas to become involved. Money was raised to improve schoolyards and parks with new equipment and plants, so that city children would care more for their surroundings.

She took people on bus tours of areas that needed work or had already been planted, often with donations she had convinced someone to give. Usually, there was at least one stop where she could get out and plant a dogwood or daffodil bulb herself. She also met with several mayors to learn what the problems were in their cities and to discuss solutions.

One of her main goals was to get rid of billboards along highways. So many commercial interests opposed her that Bill Mauldin of the *Chicago Sun-Times* once drew a cartoon showing a road lined with signs, one of which read, "Impeach Lady Bird." Eventually, thanks in part to her husband's legendary ability to twist arms, Congress did pass the Highway Beautification Act.

In her efforts to interest Americans in the beauty of their country, Lady Bird made forty-seven trips, traveling more than 200,000 miles, from Cape Canaveral, Florida, to San Simeon, California, from New England to Texas. She climbed mountains, rode the Snake River rapids, and rafted on the Rio Grande. It was not always a popular crusade; a veterans' group once objected to the color of the tulips planted around an army memorial; yellow seemed to be a slur on their courage, so they were changed to red for the next spring. The term "not fit for pigs," used in one antilitter campaign, did not go over well with hog farmers.

Lady Bird was politically savvy enough to push for her own programs and also to advise the president, in her gentle, diplomatic way. When one of his speeches seemed to be going on too long, she might send him a note saying, "Great speech but time to stop." And, of course, he could choose to ignore it. Her greatest coup on the political scene was probably the whistle-stop tour she made through the Southern states during the 1964 campaign, the first such trip by a First Lady. It was crucial to win the South for the Democrats at a time when they were pushing for new Civil Rights legislation, and Lady Bird traveled seventeen hundred miles, making 180 stops to speak from the back of the train.

One of the grandest social functions to take place during the Johnson years was the wedding ceremony in the East Room uniting Lynda Bird and marine captain

Charles Robb, who later became governor of Virginia. Luci Baines, who had married Patrick Nugent eighteen months earlier in a Catholic ceremony, brought the first Johnson grandchild to the White House.

By 1968, fighting the war in Vietnam and the war's protesters at home had become too much for Lyndon, and he announced he would not run for another term in office. He and Lady Bird retired to their ranch in Texas where he died in 1973.

Lady Bird's account of her busy years as First Lady, *White House Diary*, was published in 1970, and in 1981 a documentary film, *The First Lady, A Portrait of Lady Bird Johnson*, was made. Her interest in the natural beauty of the country remained strong; she founded the National Wildflower Research Center in 1982 and became a member of the Board of Trustees of the National Geographic Society.

Her Beautification Committee had helped to make cleaning up and making better use of natural resources a popular issue in the sixties, and Columbia Island in the Potomac River, which is now alive with dogwoods and flowers, was renamed Lady Bird Johnson Park.

Patricia Ryan Nixon
1912–

"A GOOD SPORT"
Richard M. Nixon Administration 1969–74

❖

"I am a good sport," Pat Nixon declared, and she was indeed an amazingly good sport. Through sheer will and determination, she made the best of a life of hardships and disappointments that would have destroyed many weaker women. Through the years, she built up an impenetrable outer shell for protection, but the two women who knew her best, her daughters, describe what they saw as the real Pat Nixon: Contrary to the public image of Plastic Pat, Tricia says her mother was "outgoing, vivacious, talented and capable," and to Julie, she was "the most independent and self-sufficient woman I know . . . a woman of dignity."

Thelma Catherine Ryan was born in Ely, Nevada, on the day before St. Patrick's Day and was called Babe (his "St. Patrick's Babe in the morning") by her father,

PATRICIA RYAN NIXON

William Ryan, and two brothers. She adopted the name Pat for herself when he died. When Pat was two years old her family moved to Artesia, California, and the five-room house on an eleven-acre truck farm where she was raised. Her youth was one of hard work, helping in the fields, and school. Life became even more difficult when she was thirteen and her mother died, leaving Pat to care for her father and brothers.

When she was eighteen, her father died and Pat was on her own. After a year of junior college, she took two years off to do some traveling and chauffeured an elderly couple across the country to New York, saying later that she was "driver, nurse, mechanic—and scared." After two years in New York, she returned to California and worked her way through college, making extra money doing such things as testing hair sprays and working as a movie extra. By 1937, she had her B.S. degree from U.C.L.A. and took a job teaching shorthand and typing at Whittier (California) High School.

Such a difficult beginning to life might have produced a grim drudge, but Pat Ryan was a very attractive, finely boned, lively, warm young woman, popular with her students, interested in people, and involved in such activities as amateur theatrics. It was at the Whittier Community Players that she met struggling young lawyer Richard Nixon, who proposed to her the first time he met her. They were married two years later, in 1940.

Given her choice, Pat would probably have chosen to settle down and raise a family as the wife of a successful attorney, but when politics reared its ugly head, she once again adapted. She learned what it was to be a politician's wife in the 1940s, which meant looking enthralled at her husband's speeches, saying very little in public so as to avoid possible mistakes, traveling and being away from her children, and smiling, always smiling.

From Dick's first hard-hitting, red-baiting campaign for Congress in 1946 (in which he became known as "Tricky Dick"), Pat was right with him, spending long days in the campaign office—both before and after the birth of their first child, Tricia—sometimes as his only staff member. Through the years, politics with all its perks and privileges and financial gains came to mean everything to Dick, but to his wife they meant sacrificing all that she held dear: family, friends, privacy. Several times he wrote and signed pledges for her, promising to leave politics, but he always broke the promises.

In 1950, Dick was elected to the Senate, and two years later he was Dwight Eisenhower's vice president, putting Pat in that somewhat nebulous position of Second Lady. There wasn't much time to wonder what the wife of a vice president does; during her eight years in the position, she accompanied her husband on his travels throughout the world, visiting a total of fifty-three countries. On their tour of South America, the Nixons faced mobs of leftists in Venezuela who spat on them, threw rocks, and had plans for even more violence, which the Nixons were fortunate to have missed. Pat was extolled for her calm and courage throughout the ordeal.

When Dick lost the presidential election in 1960 to John Kennedy, Pat was a happy private citizen—until Dick decided to run for governor of California in 1962. When he lost that election and seemed to be washed up in politics, she spent six peaceful and prosperous years in an apartment on New York's Fifth Avenue. It must have taken incredible determination to once again follow her husband out on the campaign trail in 1968 and then into the White House.

As First Lady, Pat was a busy if somewhat formal hostess, more in the Eisenhower than the Kennedy style. There were evenings of entertainment featuring such luminaries as Duke Ellington, Andrew Wyeth, Isaac Stern, Leonard Bernstein, Bob Hope, and others. The Nixons also initiated Sunday-morning religious services at the White House, raising the issue of separation of church and state in the minds of some observers. An important objective with Pat was "to share the house with thousands of people." Unfortunately, although she enjoyed meeting people, she often found that her role as organizer of events was usurped by the president's domineering staff, especially H. R. Haldeman.

There were complaints that Pat did not have what the public—or at least the public press—had come to expect of a First Lady, a major project. It seemed to her, though, to be somewhat artificial to suddenly claim one overwhelming concern, when, as she had said, "people are my project." She stuck to her interest in encouraging volunteerism, personally reading and trying to reply to thousands of pieces of mail a week and being a hostess. She also arranged the details of her elder daughter's marriage to Edward Cox in the Rose Garden in June 1971. The younger daughter, Julie, had married ex-President Eisenhower's grandson, David, in 1968 in New York City.

Later unhappy events and her own reserve have probably served to obscure what may be Pat's greatest accomplishment in the White House: her acquisition of art and furniture for the public rooms. Working with executive mansion curator Clement Conger, she acquired millions of dollars' worth of antiques and paintings, including portraits of Dolley Madison and Louisa Adams, either purchased or given as gifts or as loans, and furnished the mansion with museum-quality pieces. Conger averred that she "did more for the authentic refurbishing of the White House and its beautification than any other Administration in history—and that includes the Kennedy." She also arranged to have floodlights illuminate the White House at night.

As First Lady, Pat seemed to gain in confidence and became more outgoing. This was especially evident in her trips abroad, where she seemed more warm and uninhibited, than among her own critical countrymen. She once said that "personal diplomacy" was her greatest contribution, and certainly people appreciated her most on a one-to-one basis. Her personal style was favorably noted in the press on the trips she made alone to Peru after its devastating earthquake in 1970 and to Africa in 1972. She was also given high marks for her trips with her husband to China, Russia, and South America. The media was definitely warming up to the "new" Pat Nixon.

Unfortunately, the good times were not to last; the Watergate scandal came to dominate the press after Richard's reelection in 1972, and Pat retreated behind her mask as the perfect political wife who would deny to the death that there were problems, that she was tired, that she was probably more unhappy than she had ever been. Only once in a while would her real feelings sneak out, as when she was asked whether her daughter should marry a politician. Pat replied that she "would feel sorry for her if she did." And when the reporter said, "You married one," Pat responded with the understatement, "Yes, but I don't tell everything."

Her resentment and suspicion of the "glamour boys" like the Kennedys, who seemed to have it all and to be treated kindly if not adoringly by the press, spilled over in one interview (with Gloria Steinem) when she said, "I never had time to think about things like—who I wanted to be or who I admired, or to have ideas. I never had time to dream about being anyone else. I had to work . . . I've never had it easy. I'm not like all you . . . all those people who had it easy."

It was frustrating for Pat as First Lady to be taking part in what she considered interesting or important events and to have reporters ask only about the family's reactions to the latest scandalous revelations. When some women from the Religious Broadcasters of America assured her that they were praying for her husband, Pat Nixon reminded them to "pray for the press," too.

The discovery of damaging tapes of executive office conversations was the final straw. Nixon had not felt as Pat did, that the tapes should be destroyed "because they were like a private diary, not public property." By August 1974, it was all over; Nixon became the first American president to resign. He and Pat turned the White House over to Vice President Ford and returned to their home on the Pacific Ocean, San Clemente, from which they seldom ventured for many bleak months. Then, in the spring of 1975, Pat returned to Artesia to be present at the dedication of the Patricia Nixon Elementary School. When she spoke to the group there, she told them that schools were usually named for people who were gone, then added, "I am happy to tell you that I'm not gone—I mean not really gone."

In 1976, Dick was disbarred from the practice of law, and devastating personal accusations about Pat's "drinking heavily" and her loveless marriage were published in Woodward and Bernstein's *The Final Days*. That summer, Pat suffered her first stroke. Four years later, the Nixons moved east to be near their daughters and four grandchildren. Pat's health was poor—she had another minor stroke in 1983—but she was living the private life she always wanted, filled with family, gardening, and reading. In 1986, Julie's book, *Pat Nixon, The Untold Story*, presented an admiring portrait of her indomitable mother.

Pat Nixon had said that she just wanted to go down in history "as the wife of the President," and she probably will. But she will also be remembered and admired as one of the most stoically loyal women ever to reside in the White House.

Elizabeth Bloomer Warren Ford
1918–

"WOMAN OF CANDOR"
Gerald R. Ford Administration 1974–77

❖

Even the Democrats liked Betty Ford. Her openness and joie de vivre were a welcome sign that a First Lady didn't really have to pack her personality in cotton and store it in a drawer until she moved out of the White House. Betty claimed that she was just "an ordinary woman who was called on stage at an extraordinary time. I was no different once I became First Lady than I had been before." Being "no different" may be what made her so special.

Betty was born to Hortense Neahr and William Bloomer in Chicago, Illinois, in 1918 and was raised in Grand Rapids, Michigan. At sixteen, she lost her father;

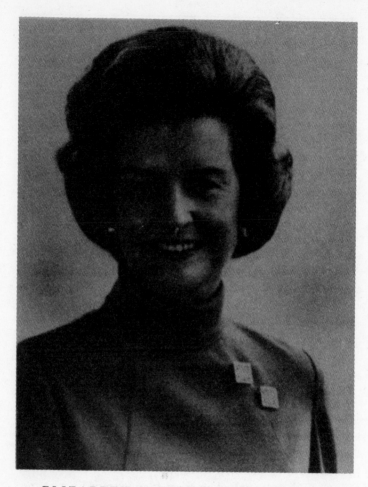

ELIZABETH BLOOMER WARREN FORD

while repairing his car in a closed garage, Bloomer succumbed to carbon monoxide fumes.

Dancing was Betty's first love, her "happiness," starting with classes in social dancing in her hometown when she was eight. By the time she was a teenager, she was teaching dance herself. At eighteen, she left home for the first time to spend the summer at the Bennington School of Dance in Vermont, where she studied for two summers. She met the legendary Martha Graham there and studied dance choreography with her in New York for two years.

Back home again, she gave dance lessons, worked as a fashion coordinator at a department store, had a five-year marriage to a hometown man that ended in divorce, and met rising young politician Jerry Ford. The month after they were married in 1948, he was elected to the House of Representatives. They moved to Washington and stayed there for the next twenty-eight years.

The life of a congressman's wife was a difficult one. It was not uncommon for Jerry to be away from home for two hundred days of the year, leaving Betty to raise their four children—three sons and a daughter—and handle the details of their household in the capital's suburbs. There was little time for dancing or pursuing her interest in fashion, and the stress and loneliness took their toll. Many years later, she revealed that during those years she had developed a pinched nerve in her neck and for a while was drinking more than she should have. Finally, there was a complete breakdown, and she began seeing a psychiatrist twice a week in an attempt to recover what she thought she'd lost, her "feeling of self-worth."

In October 1973, President Nixon's vice president, Spiro Agnew, resigned in a cloud of scandal over kickbacks. As Watergate disclosures mounted, someone "squeaky clean" was desperately needed to take Agnew's place. Jerry Ford fit the bill.

The new vice president's wife immediately entered the media spotlight. During a television interview, she was asked if she agreed with the Supreme Court's ruling on abortion, and Betty responded positively, saying, "It was time to bring abortion out of the backwoods and put it in the hospitals where it belonged." After that the lines were drawn. The people who applauded her honesty outnumbered her critics, but she had to learn to live with both.

On August 9, 1974, Nixon resigned, and the Michigan congressman leapfrogged into the presidency. And his First Lady's reputation for candor was firmly established when she let it be known that they would not have separate bedrooms. Judging from some of the reaction to that statement, one might think that presidents were supposed to take a vow of celibacy. Less than two months later, Betty made more serious news when it was announced that she had entered the hospital because of a lump on one breast. It turned out to be malignant and a mastectomy was required. Her openness on this subject convinced thousands of other women to have breast examinations. One of these was Happy Rockefeller, the wife of the new vice president; she had the same operation about a month later.

Betty may have been partly right when she said that she only seemed outspoken because her predecessor, Pat Nixon, had been so quiet, but there have been few First

Ladies who seemed so loath to sidestep the often imperti-
nent questions that came her way. And Jerry was not the
type of husband who put a gag on his wife's opinions. In
another television interview, she confessed that she
would not be surprised if their unmarried daughter,
Susan, were to have an affair, although she would want
to know if the man "were nice or not." Questioned on
whether any of her children had ever smoked marijuana,
Betty said she assumed that they had probably experi-
mented with it.

Behind the scenes, too, the First Lady made people
aware of her opinions. She phoned and wrote legislators
in support of the Equal Rights Amendment, while the
opposition picketed the White House with placards
reading, "Betty Ford, Get Off the Phone." She also used
her unlimited access to the president to encourage the
appointment of women to high places and was disappointed that a woman was not appointed to the Supreme
Court during her husband's tenure. She was pleased that
he named Anne Armstrong to the position of ambassador
to Great Britain, and even would have liked Armstrong
to be Jerry's running mate in 1976, but pillow talk only
goes so far.

The Ford White House was more relaxed, less regal
than many before it. As a hostess, Betty was inclined to
make entertainment less formal, using small round tables
and eliminating some of the courses at official dinners.
Only five days after becoming First Lady, she had to be
the hostess for a state dinner for King Hussein of Jordan.
Everything went smoothly (with the usual help from the
White House staff), and the amiability of both host and
hostess created a festive atmosphere; the king was heard

to say it was "the most enjoyable party" he had attended at the White House.

At such affairs, the Fords loved to dance and mingle with the guests, often staying long after dinner. There were some who found them frivolous, but the First Lady wisely ignored the critics, contending that dancing "was part of [their] hospitality."

During her two and a half years in the White House, Betty also played hostess to England's Queen Elizabeth, President Anwar Sadat of Egypt, Queen Margrethe of Denmark, the Emperor and Empress of Japan, and Prime Minister Liam Cosgrave of Ireland. In their travels abroad, the Fords received the royal treatment in Europe, Indonesia, the Philippines, and China. In Peking, Betty made a hit by dancing in her stocking feet with the young students of a ballet school.

When 1976 rolled around, Jerry decided he wanted to stay in the White House. Betty had rather hoped that they would finally retire from politics, but she gamely joined him on the campaign trail. The public's enthusiasm for her was sometimes greater than it was for her husband; many people wore campaign buttons reading, "Keep Betty in the White House" or "Elect Betty's Husband." But even she couldn't win it for him.

Retired and living in Palm Springs, Betty Ford continued to make news. In the spring of 1978, she opened up her life once again and told the world that she had a drug and alcohol dependency and entered a rehabilitation program. Her new awareness of the problems of chemical dependency led to the creation of the Betty Ford Center for its treatment, and she began to spend most of her time working on alcoholism and trying to remove its stigma.

Later that year, Betty decided to have a new face to go with her new life and told the world about her face lift, as if it wouldn't have noticed.

Her memoirs, *The Times of My Life*, were published in 1978 and a few years later were used as the basis for a television drama about her White House years and her struggle with addiction. In 1987, her new book, *Betty; A Glad Awakening*, was published.

Jerry Ford may not go down in history as one of our strongest presidents, but Betty will be long remembered as one of the country's most interesting, outspoken, and influential First Ladies. By the time she left the White House, the country knew her views on abortion and the E.R.A. They knew how much she loved dancing and smart clothes. They knew all about her chronic tardiness, her divorce, her psychiatric treatment, her mastectomy, and her alcohol and drug problem.

Does being so open about one's life mean that a woman is a feminist? Not necessarily. It sort of depends on what a woman is open about. There are those who would say that having a face lift is encouraging sexism and ageism. Maybe so, but it was just another instance of this woman in a prominent position saying to others of her sex that it's not shameful to feel so pressured and unappreciated that you need psychiatric help, that you can live a full and feminine life after breast surgery, that you can speak your own mind even if your husband doesn't agree, that alcoholism is not a crime and can be treated, and that if having a new face makes you feel better, well then, why not.

Rosalynn Smith Carter
1927–

"STEEL MAGNOLIA"
Jimmy Carter Administration 1977–81

Almost two hundred years after John and Abigail Adams occupied the White House, there appeared on the political scene the very similar partnership of Jimmy and Rosalynn Smith Carter of Plains, Georgia. Like the Adamses, the Carters collaborated on family, business, and politics. And, most would agree, like Abigail, Rosalynn was a very politically involved First Lady— perhaps the most active since Eleanor Roosevelt.

When Rosalynn was thirteen, her father, a mechanic, died, and as the oldest of four children, she took on many responsibilities to help her mother around the house. By fifteen, she was bringing money home from a job in a beauty parlor. She managed to go on to Georgia Southwestern College as a day student. Then, in 1945, midshipman James Earl Carter, home on leave from the

ROSALYNN SMITH CARTER

U.S. Naval Academy at Annapolis, Maryland, finally
noticed the pretty, slender, dark-haired seventeen-year-
old—as she had hoped he would for several years. They
were married a year later.

One of Rosalynn's ambitions had always been to leave
her small town, and marriage to a naval officer now made
that possible. They were stationed in New York, Connecticut, and Hawaii. As her family expanded—with the
birth of three sons—so did her world. And as she coped
successfully with the details of many moves, she grew in
confidence.

For Rosalynn, the lowest point in the Carter marriage
came when Jimmy's father died and Jimmy decided to
leave the navy and take charge of the family peanut
warehouse business back in Plains. She was, at first,
miserable about having to return to small town life. Then
one day she went down to the warehouse and looked over
the books, which needed work. She studied accounting
on her own and within a few years knew more about the
financial aspects of the business than her husband.

The Carters also became more involved in community
affairs, then local and state politics. Rosalynn first
learned about campaigning when Jimmy ran for and won
a race for state senator. She enjoyed managing the family
and the business during the months he spent in Atlanta.
She felt she was "contributing to our life and making it
possible for him to pursue a political career. I was more a
political partner than a political wife."

In 1967, when Rosalynn was forty years old, the
Carters had a daughter, Amy, who saw her parents go
off to campaign for the Georgia governorship when she
was two years old. Rosalynn traveled across the state,

fighting off a shyness that could still make her physically ill when she had to give a speech.

Being first lady in the governor's mansion for four years was good training for a woman destined to go on to the White House. Her predecessor, Mrs. Lester Maddox, had cooked official dinners herself, shaken hands with every tourist who traipsed through the governor's mansion six days a week, and never had an office of her own. That was not for Rosalynn. She felt that she should take advantage of a first lady's ability to "pick and choose her projects and do almost anything she wants because her name is a drawing card, she is influential and . . . she also has access to the press."

One of her first priorities was to improve services to the mentally and emotionally handicapped, and she attended meetings, volunteered at and toured hospitals, and helped put together the final proposals for change. She also supported the Equal Rights Amendment and worked on state beautification projects.

Four years later, it was back on the campaign trail—this time nationwide—and Jimmy gave his wife, his "secret weapon," full credit for her part in their successful race for the presidency: "Rosalynn and I were the ones that discussed every facet of the prospective campaign. . . . She can do everything as well as I can." Her sensitivity to the feelings of people helped to form his positions, and he always claimed that she was a "full partner or better."

From wherever Rosalynn was campaigning, she would check in with her husband to give him feedback and practical advice. She urged him to stop gesturing in the "V" sign, too reminiscent of Nixon. She pinpointed key states in which she felt Jimmy should make personal appearances and suggested points of emphasis for his speeches. In some ways, her sense of political timing and her facility for the *mot juste* were sharper than Jimmy's; she would surely have advised against his calculated candor in admitting to lusting in his heart for other women, as he did to a *Playboy* magazine reporter.

Once in the White House (1976), Rosalynn discovered the truth: "The role of First Lady is a difficult—and sometimes nearly impossible—one to fill." Like all her predecessors, she had to find her own way to handle it, and her way was as an activist. In 1977, for example, some of her activities included: 71 travel days visiting 16 countries and 21 U.S. cities; 227 hours attending public and private meetings; 250 hours spent on her mental health projects; 71 hours in briefing sessions; 210 hours learning Spanish; and uncounted hours involved in 39 receptions, 20 congressional leadership breakfasts, 15 luncheons, 8 state dinners, 8 picnics, and 19 arrival ceremonies for visiting dignitaries. During a visit with Mamie Eisenhower, after the two women had compared their experiences, the older woman exclaimed, "I stayed busy all the time and loved being in the White House, but I was never expected to do all the things you have to do."

Rosalynn enjoyed the social life in the White House. She was briefed on the interests of heads of state who were guests so that entertaining could be personalized. And she liked to have picnics on the South Lawn in summer; in 1979, she held a dinner for eighteen hundred there to celebrate the signing of the Middle East peace treaty. She arranged to have the performances of such artists as pianist Vladimir Horowitz, cellist Mstislav Rostropovich, soprano Leontyne Price, and guitarist Andrés Segovia broadcast on public television so that everyone could enjoy them. Some of the changes she made included: serving only wine, sharing the reviewing stand with wives of dignitaries instead of standing in the background, and having women included in the honor guard for the first time.

Rosalynn was not overly concerned with her wardrobe (she wore a six-year-old gown to the inaugural ball), decorating, or china. Much more to her liking was traveling to the Caribbean and Latin America on a fourteen-day diplomatic mission and doing whatever she could to make the "Camp David accord" between Egypt and Israel a reality. She was the second First Lady called to testify—on mental health legislation—before a senate committee (Eleanor Roosevelt having been the first).

Critics have called Rosalynn cold and calculating, labeling her the "steel magnolia." One of the reasons for this seeming toughness was the result of her attempt to overcome her shyness, but it went deeper than that. Like Sarah Polk and Abigail Adams, Rosalynn felt that the country really needed her husband's leadership, and she was determined to help make him president, to work with him on the job, and to present her side of things to the media.

She scheduled a weekly White House lunch with Jimmy on Wednesdays so they could discuss and make decisions on family, financial, and political issues they were working on in common. This left his evenings free from decision making. When she attended cabinet meetings in an attempt to become well informed without having to plow through piles of paperwork, it provoked such an outcry that one might have thought she was a member of the KGB. She viewed the criticism of her active involvement philosophically, "I had already learned . . . that I was going to be criticized no matter what I did, so I might as well be criticized for something I wanted to do."

The Carters discussed everything together. She assumed the adviser's role in areas where she had become especially knowledgeable, such as mental health, women's issues, and care for the elderly. And when Jimmy was to make an important speech about a subject not in her field, such as energy, she "went over it line by line with him," because she "thought if I could understand it, then everybody could understand it." Presidential advisers who despaired of making Jimmy see things their way would appeal to Rosalynn to plead their cause, knowing the influence she had. Speaking to a group in Spokane, Washington, about the recommendations in the mental health report, Jimmy admitted that "the best lobbyist in the United States will be there with me every day and alongside me every night."

In 1979, the year before Jimmy hoped to be reelected, Iranian militants overran the U.S. embassy in Tehran and took everyone there hostage. They were held throughout the election year, making Jimmy himself a hostage, as he refrained from campaigning until the situation was resolved. But by the time the hostages came home, the Carters had lost to the Reagans and were back in Plains.

Rosalynn continued to put her energies into working to improve mental health services, became involved in

Friendship Force to promote understanding between people of different nationalities, and was active in the Habitat for Humanity program in which volunteers help in building homes for the poor. She spent two and a half years writing her best-selling book, *First Lady from Plains*, published in 1984, and collaborated with Jimmy on *Everything to Gain: Making the Most of the Rest of Your Life*, published in 1987.

Rosalynn's term as First Lady raised old questions about the role of unelected relatives and their accountability to the American public. Obviously the jury is still out—and not expected to return in the near future.

"Nancy" Robbins Davis Reagan
1921–

"DRAGON LADY"
Ronald Reagan Administration 1981–

❖

Nancy Reagan came from a show business background, and she brought some of the glamour with her to Washington. Her sets were lavish, her wardrobe expensive, and her costar was handsome. Only her role was ill-conceived and had to be rewritten.

Nancy was born Anne Frances Robbins in 1921—or as she claims in her autobiography, 1923—the daughter of actress Edith Luckett. Her father, Kenneth Robbins, left mother and daughter soon after the birth and was seldom seen again. Anne Frances lived with relatives in Maryland for six years while her mother toured with the theater. When she was almost eight, her mother married Chicago neurosurgeon Dr. Loyal Davis, and Anne

"NANCY" ROBBINS DAVIS REAGAN

Frances Robbins became Nancy (her mother's nickname for her) Davis (when Dr. Davis adopted her at fourteen). She became a part of the world of wealth and privilege, had a coming-out party, and graduated from Smith College.

With some help from her mother's theater friends, such as Zasu Pitts and Spencer Tracy, Nancy appeared in some small parts on Broadway; then, in 1949, she signed with M.G.M. in Hollywood, where she played girl-next-door roles usually assigned to wholesome, prim-looking young women. Her first big part was in *East Side, West Side*; her last movie, in 1957, was *Hellcats of the Navy*, in which she appeared with her husband, Ronald Reagan. The Reagans had met in 1949 when he was president of the Screen Actors Guild, and she wanted to discuss a problem with him. They were married in 1952.

Ronald, after quitting the Democratic party, was elected Republican governor of California in 1966. As the governor's wife, Nancy was criticized for the same things that would haunt her twenty years later in the White House: her friends were all wealthy society women or Hollywood types only interested in fashion; she interfered with Ronald's work, phoning and insisting on speaking with him even when he was in conference; made demands of his aides and arranged his schedules; and when she watched her husband in public, it was with an expression in her huge hazel eyes that became known as "the Gaze." Political reporter Lou Cannon described it as "a kind of transfixed adoration more appropriate to a witness of the Virgin Birth."

The press continued to be severe on Nancy when Ronald was elected president in 1980. To tell her side of the story, she wrote her autobiography, *Nancy*, but that didn't answer all the questions either, such as those about the rebellious Reagan children, Patricia and Ron, who refused to campaign for their father and were often opposed to his positions on subjects such as Vietnam and nuclear energy. Even before the inauguration, the First Lady–elect was taken to task for apparently hinting that the Carters should move out of the White House early so she could begin redecorating. Then she received bad notices for the thousands of dollars her inaugural gowns cost and for having her hairdressers flown in to secure the placement of each hair.

Feminists were upset by her opposition to the E.R.A. and abortion and by her apparent lack of any goals for herself. Any time not spent on redecorating, Nancy vowed to spend "supporting him." Gloria Steinem considered her the perfect "Marzipan Wife," that "rare woman who can perform the miracle of having no interests at all; of transplanting her considerable ego into a male body." Betty Friedan complained that Nancy "has not advanced the cause of women at all."

Nancy's image was also hurt by revelations that, thanks to tax-deductible gifts from her wealthy friends, she was able to spend more than $800,000 on redoing the White House family quarters. Though the china she ordered—220 place settings at a cost of over $200,000— had been a gift from an anonymous donor, such materialistic preoccupations brought public outcry—especially since the administration was calling for sacrifices and counting catsup as a vegetable in lunch menus for underprivileged schoolchildren.

Clearly something had to be done about Nancy's image; no longer could she be "more interested in being socially chic than socially useful." In her second year as First Lady, she decided to make her interest in drug abuse by young people her project and began to travel and speak to groups at schools and drug-treatment centers. In 1983, she narrated a public television program "The Chemical People" and started the "Just Say No" to drugs campaign. She also appeared as herself on a television situation comedy in which she appealed to teenagers not to use drugs. In 1986, Ronald joined her for a twenty-minute television pitch for a "National Crusade for a Drug-Free America."

As might be expected, entertaining in the Reagan White House was more formal than it had been with the Carters; white-tie diplomatic receptions were revived and liquor was brought back. Royalty and heads of state mixed with Hollywood luminaries. The brightest affair may have been the 1985 visit of the English royal couple, Prince Charles and Princess Diana.

The nightmare of every president's wife became reality for Nancy in March 1981 when Ronald was shot by a mentally disturbed young man seeking recognition from an actress he admired. Fortunately, Ronald Reagan was the first president to be shot and survive. In 1985, there was another scare when the president underwent surgery for colon cancer, but again he pulled through and returned to work.

A year later, an "autobiographical novel" by their

daughter, Patricia, was published; in it she described a strained family situation with a preoccupied father and a rigid mother. And young Ron appeared in his underwear in a skit on a late-night comedy show. The Reagan children were still going their own way.

Nancy will probably not be remembered for her designer dresses or her china purchase or her problems with her children or even her antidrug program. Historians will surely be more interested in discussing just how much power this First Lady wielded and what were the effects of that power.

First there was the question of whether she—having come from the home of a very conservative Republican stepfather—had anything to do with Ronald's switch from the Democratic party to the conservative wing of the Republicans. She denied it, saying, "I didn't know anything about politics when we got married. . . . I couldn't have changed anybody to anything."

Still, there was no denying that she sometimes fed him his lines. During the 1980 campaign, when a reporter asked Ronnie a question about marijuana, Nancy was heard to prompt him, "Tell him you wouldn't know," and Ron turned around and used the line. Five years later, when he seemed to hesitate about answering a question about arms control, Nancy again quietly cued him with the response, "We're doing everything we can."

Most observers would agree that the First Lady was not involved in policy-making, though she confessed that she "might suggest an idea to him"; her influence seemed to be strongest in matters of personnel and scheduling. Her opinion about people carried some weight with her husband because, as she admitted, "I think maybe I'm a little bit more attuned to who might be good or loyal or whatever." Ronald's aides knew that it paid to be on her good side, because, as one said, "if she likes someone, it can help. If she doesn't think much of someone, it can hurt." It was also "much easier to get him to go along" if Nancy agreed with an idea.

She also paid close attention to what his staff had on the schedule for the president, insisting that he not "overdo" and become tired. This was especially true after he had been in the hospital.

All her influence—or power or meddling—came roaring into the public consciousness in 1987 because of a combination of more surgery (prostate) for Ronnie, exposure of the sale of weapons by the administration to a terrorist nation (Iran), and the use of profits from the sale to arm a group Congress had voted to cut off (the Contras). In her efforts to protect him and keep his scheduling light during convalescence and to effect changes in the people advising him, Nancy became known as the "Dragon Lady." The president called the accusations of her taking charge of the government "despicable fiction," but details of her technique of using leaks to the press and passing requests to a circle of friends and advisers became public, and suddenly she was as unpopular as she had been in her first year in the White House.

After six years on the job, however, Nancy Reagan had learned a few things and could defend herself. She used humor in a speech in New York, when she told the audience how busy she was "staffing the White House and overseeing the arms talks," then laid it on the line:

NANCY ROBBINS DAVIS REAGAN

"It's silly to suggest my opinion should not carry some weight with a man I've been married to for thirty-five years . . . and I make no apologies for looking out for his personal and political welfare." She also defended the right of a political spouse to hold an opinion and express it.

Ironically, this model of womanhood, who once said her life began when she married Ronald Reagan, and who dedicated that life to his well-being and to seeing that he had what she considered his rightful place in history, may go down in history as one of this country's most powerful First Ladies—not in spite of her devotion but because of it.

DIANA DIXON HEALY, author of *America's Vice Presidents*, lives in Wilton, Connecticut, with her husband, Charles, and their three sons.

CHRISTIAN HERALD
People Making A Difference

Christian Herald is a family of dedicated, Christ-centered ministries that reaches out to deprived children in need, and to homeless men who are lost in alcoholism and drug addiction. Christian Herald also offers the finest in family and evangelical literature through its book clubs and publishes a popular, dynamic magazine for today's Christians.

Our Ministries

Family Bookshelf and **Christian Bookshelf** provide a wide selection of inspirational reading and Christian literature written by best-selling authors. All books are recommended by an Advisory Board of distinguished writers and editors.

Christian Herald magazine is contemporary, a dynamic publication that addresses the vital concerns of today's Christian. Each monthly issue contains a sharing of true personal stories written by people who have found in Christ the strength to make a difference in the world around them.

Christian Herald Children. The door of God's grace opens wide to give impoverished youngsters a breath of fresh air, away from the evils of the streets. Every summer, hundreds of youngsters are welcomed at the Christian Herald Mont Lawn Camp located in the Poconos at Bushkill, Pennsylvania. Year-round assistance is also provided, including teen programs, tutoring in reading and writing, family counseling, career guidance and college scholarship programs.

The Bowery Mission. Located in New York City, the Bowery Mission offers hope and Gospel strength to the downtrodden and homeless. Here, the men of Skid Row are fed, clothed, ministered to. Many voluntarily enter a 6-month discipleship program of spiritual guidance, nutrition therapy and Bible study.

Our Father's House. Located in rural Pennsylvania, Our Father's House is a discipleship and job training center. Alcoholics and drug addicts are given an opportunity to recover, away from the temptations of city streets.

Christian Herald ministries, founded in 1878, are supported by the voluntary contributions of individuals and by legacies and bequests. Contributions are tax deductible. Checks should be made out to Christian Herald Children, The Bowery Mission, or to Christian Herald Association.

Administrative Office: 40 Overlook Drive, Chappaqua, New York 10514
Telephone: (914) 769-9000

Fully accredited Member
of the Evangelical Council
for Financial Accountability

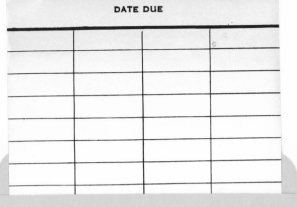